Your 30-Day Devotional to Ignite Biblical Prayer against Spiritual Warfare

Marta E. Greenman & Maureen H. Maldonado

PrayerFULL

Marta E. Greenman

&

Maureen H. Maldonado

© 2024 Marta E. Greenman and Maureen H. Maldonado

Published by Words of Grace & Truth PO Box 860223 Plano, TX 75086.

(469) 854-3574

Words of Grace & Truth is honored to present this title in partnership with the authors. The views expressed or implied in this work are those of the authors. Words of Grace & Truth provides our imprint seal representing design excellence, creative content, and high-quality production.

No part of this publication may be reproduced, stored in a retrieval system, or transmitted in any way by any means—electronic, mechanical, photocopy, recording, or otherwise—without the prior permission of the copyright holder, except as provided by US copyright law.

The authors have permission to use all versions noted in *PrayerFULL: Your 30-Day Devotional to Ignite Biblical Prayer against Spiritual Warfare*

Unless otherwise noted, Scripture quotations are taken from the New American Standard Bible © Copyright 1960, 1962, 1963, 1968, 1971, 1972, 1973, 1975, 1977, 1995 by The Lockman Foundation. Used by permission.

Scripture quotations from The ESV® Bible (The Holy Bible, English Standard Version®), © 2001 by Crossway, a publishing ministry of Good News Publishers. Used by permission. All rights reserved.

ISBN Softcover Color: 978-1-960575-22-7
ISBN Hardcover Color: 978-1-960575-24-1
ISBN Softcover B&W: 978-1-960575-23-4
ISBN Kindle: 978-1-960575-25-8
ISBN Audio Book: 978-1-960575-26-5
Library of Congress Catalog Number: 2024909727

ACKNOWLEDGMENTS

To Becky, I have no idea how many hours you have prayed for me and the ministry of Words of Grace & Truth, may the Lord bless you indeed. Your prayers are not taken for granted.

To Maureen, what a joy to call you friend, I look forward to many more hours of prayers together. You are a treasure from the Lord.

To my mother, Lillie, thanks for your prayers and unending love.

To my brother, Tim, I can't imagine how many prayers you have prayed for me and our family. Thank you for your faithfulness.

To my husband, Marshall, thanks for your love and daily attention.

To my Lord and Savior, *El Shama*, my God who hears and answers every prayer.

Marta E Greenman

To Jesus, You are the answer to all prayer.

To Marta, my friend, mentor, and true inspiration.

To my family for giving me reasons every day to laugh, love, and pray.

To my husband, Ray, thank you for continually supporting me on this journey called life.

To you, the reader, for being willing to spend time to learn new ways to pray!

Maureen H Maldonado

PHOTO CREDITS

Alana Brown, Magan Nguyen, Cody Ogg Photography

FORWARD

The Lord called me to pray in 1993 and I have spent the last thirty years and hours a day studying the Word of God. I searched His Word to teach me how to pray and to see answers to prayers so I could praise Him!

PrayerFULL: Your 30-Day Devotional to Ignite Biblical Prayer against Spiritual Warfare is one of the most amazing 30-Day Devotionals I have ever read. This devotional will give you a roadmap to pray and study God's Word to enrich your life.

Why do you pray?

Who do you pray to?

Do you expect answers to your prayers?

Only you can answer these questions and this devotional will be your guide as you walk through the next thirty days. Please share this study with everyone! May the Lord bless you as you read, study, and pray this incredible 30-Day journal.

May it be so.
In the mighty name of Jesus Christ, my beloved Lord.

Becky Hudson
Prayer Ambassador
Words of Grace & Truth

"Do not be anxious about anything, but in everything by prayer and pleading with thanksgiving let your requests be made known to God" (Philippians 4:6).

TABLE OF CONTENTS

Introducing Marta and Maureen 11
Authors' Note 15
Instructions 17

Section One: Old Testament

Za'aq 20
OUR STORY: *Pray About Everything! - Part 1* 23
OUR STORY: *Pray About Everything! - Part 2* 25
DAY 1 - PRAYER FOR HELP IN TIME OF TROUBLE - Psalm 142:1-7 29
Nā' 35
DAY 2 - PRAYER FOR THE REBELLIOUS - Numbers 14:11-19 37
Qārā' 45
DAY 3 - PRAYER OF JABEZ - 1 Chronicles 4:10 47
Pāl'al 55
DAY 4 - PRAYER OF THE AFFLICTED - 1 Samuel 1:10-11 57
DAY 5 - PRAYER OF REJOICING - 1 Samuel 2:1-10 63
MY STORY: Answered Prayer 69
DAY 6 - PRAYER FOR PHYSICAL HEALING - 2 Kings 20:1-11 73
DAY 7 - PRAYER OF DISTRESS - Nehemiah 1:4-11 79
DAY 8 - PRAYER OF THE REBELLIOUS PART 1 - Jonah 2:1-10 85
DAY 9 - PRAYER OF THE REBELLIOUS PART 2 - Jonah 4:2-3 91
MY STORY: Power of Praying Parents 97
ATTITUDINAL PRAYERS 101
DAY 10 - PRAYER FOR WISDOM - 1 Kings 3:5-10 103
DAY 11 - PRAYER OF DEDICATION - 1 Kings 8:22-24 109
DAY 12 - PRAYER OF PROTECTION - Psalm 25:16-22 115
MY STORY: Praying for a Miracle 121
DAY 13 - PRAYER OF REPENTANCE AND RESTORATION - Psalm 51 125
DAY 14 - PRAYER OF PRAISE AND REMEMBRANCE - Psalm 103:1-14 .. 131
DAY 15 - PRAYER OF THANKSGIVING - Psalm 118:1-4; 15-14 137

Section 2: New Testament

Aitema 144
OUR STORY: *Becoming PrayerFULL - Part 1* 147
OUR STORY: *Becoming PrayerFULL - Part 2* 151
DAY 16 - PRAY ABOUT EVERYTHING - Philippians 4:4-9 155
Deomai 160
DAY 17 - PRAYER OF BOLDNESS - Acts 4:24-31 163
Proseuche 168
DAY 18 - PRAYER OF THE FAITHFUL - Acts 12:5,12 171
DAY 19 - PRAYER FOR THOSE IN AUTHORITY - 1 Timothy 2:1-8 ... 177
Proseuchomai 182
MY STORY: Praying Grandmas 185
DAY 20 - THE LORD'S PRAYER - Matthew 6:7-13 189
DAY 21 - PRAYING THE FATHER'S WILL - Matthew 26:39-42 195
DAY 22 - PRAYER FOR THE PERSECUTED AND THE PERSECUTOR - Act 9:11-12 ... 201
MY STORY: Somebody's Praying for Me 209
DAY 23 - PRAYER OF PRAISE - Acts 16:23-26 213
DAY 24 - PRAYER FOR KNOWLEDGE AND SPIRITUAL WISDOM - Colossians 1:9-12 ... 219
ATTITUDINAL PRAYERS 225
DAY 25 - PRAYER OF FORGIVENESS - Luke 23:34 227
HIGH PRIESTLY PRAYER DAYS 26, 27, 28, 29 233
DAY 26 - HIGH PRIESTLY PRAYER PART 1 - Prayer of Glorification - John 17:1-10 ... 237
DAY 27 - HIGH PRIESTLY PRAYER PART 2 - Prayer of Preservation - John 17:11-16 ... 243
DAY 28 - HIGH PRIESTLY PRAYER PART 3 - Prayer of Sanctification - John 17:17-19 ... 249
DAY 29 - HIGH PRIESTLY PRAYER PART 4 - Prayer of Unification - John 17:20-26 ... 255
MY STORY: Praying Unites our Souls 261
DAY 30 - PRAYER FOR JERUSALEM - Revelation 22:20 265
YOUR STORY 270

INTRODUCING
MARTA AND MAUREEN
Marta E. Greenman

Marta left corporate America in 1998 to become a staff missionary with a church-planting organization known today as e3 Partners. She was on the American team that led international church partners in church planting. During this period, Marta spent much of her time in the field of evangelism and discipleship, traveling to Colombia, Mexico, Moldova, Peru, Romania, Ukraine, Venezuela, and Zimbabwe. She also had the privilege of leading women's conferences in biblical training.

Before Marta began writing Biblical material, she taught inductive Bible study faithfully at her home church for 15 years. Debbie Stuart, her women's ministry director, said, "Marta Greenman is a master teacher, weaving biblical principles, personal stories, and clear application with every lesson. She walks in truth, loves the Word, and has dedicated her life to teaching that truth to women."

After seven years in Romania, the Lord led Marta to write Bible studies. Her first, *Bound to Be Free*, was published in 2011. That was the same year she founded Words of Grace & Truth, a ministry devoted to teaching God's Word to the nations and teaching others to do the same, using the curriculum God birthed through her teaching ministry.

Two additional Bible studies, *Leaders, Nations, and God,* and *ACTs420NOW*, have been published since then. Marta's latest project is co-authoring 30-day devotionals, *FearLESS, LoveMORE*, and *HopeFULL* with her dear friend, Maureen Maldonado. *PrayerFULL: Your 30-Day Devotional to Ignite Biblical Prayer Against Spiritual Warfare* is the fourth in a series of 12.

GraceAndTruthRadio.World (GTRW) is a global radio station outreach with God's message of grace and truth, begun by the ministry in 2018. Marta's program, *Under God*, with co-host Maureen Maldonado, airs on GTRW Mondays at 3:30 p.m. CST. Marta's passion, regardless of the nation where she may be, is teaching God's Word and equipping others to lead. She is a gifted teacher, speaker, and expositor of God's Word. Marta lives in the Dallas–Fort Worth area with Marshall, her husband of 30 years.

Maureen H. Maldonado

Maureen, the second of seven children, grew up in a home without worldly wealth, yet she always felt treasured by her parents and knew she was rich in love. Maureen married young and raised two amazing daughters. Her grandchildren are a blessing beyond her imagination. Recently, she added two granddaughters-in-love who brought more joy to the mix. And the best yet, God blessed her with her first great-granddaughter!

Maureen has a master's degree in education from California State University and spent her career as a teacher, vice-principal, and principal in elementary education. Maureen never planned to leave California or the education system, but God had other plans.

When Maureen's husband was transferred to Arizona, then to Texas, she spent several years teaching Just Moved, a Christian program developed by Susan Miller for women who had to relocate because of life changes (*https://justmoved.org*). God used her teaching background as training to prepare Maureen for His continuing plan.

Involved in Bible studies in California, Arizona, and Texas, Maureen grew exponentially in her faith and love of God and His Word. The culmination of these experiences led her to co-host the radio program 'Under God' on GraceAndTruthRadio.World, where God's Word is taught to the nations.

Today, Maureen is using her new-to-her method of studying the Bible and her long-applied teaching methods to teach the next generation of believers. Her prayer is for others to gain as much insight into God's transformational Word as she has received. She describes it as "opening the shades and letting in all the sunlight on a gloomy day." Maureen feels honored and humbled to be a part of *Words of Grace & Truth* and asks others to join in prayer for this needed ministry, the church, our country, and our world. Maureen has co-authored with Marta three additional devotionals. Their first devotional, *FearLESS: God is calling you to be fearless and to fear less;* Second, *LoveMORE: Your 30-Day Devotional to Learn to Love like Jesus;* the third *HopeFULL: Your 30-Day Devotional to Discover Biblical Hope. PrayerFULL: Your 30-Day Devotional to Ignite Biblical Prayer Against Spiritual Warfare* is the fourth devotional.

Maureen and her husband, Raymond, reside in the Dallas–Fort Worth area where they have transplanted most of their family from California.

AUTHORS' NOTE

"You can do more than pray after you have prayed; but you can never do more than pray until you have prayed." A.J. Gordon

Dear Reader,

Prayer is our first weapon of warfare when it comes to winning any victory in this, our temporary home. Jim Reeves wrote a song, *This World Is Not My Home*. It begins with, *"This world is not my home, I'm just a-passing through,"* and ends with, *"I can't feel at home in this world anymore."* If you're as concerned as Maureen and me about the destruction and chaos in the world, you can relate to the songwriter's message. Yet, we are here because God has kept us for His divine purpose.

Over the next 30 days, we will examine prayers in the Bible. We want you to learn how to pray God's Word and incorporate this precious tool into your prayer life. We all want our petitions to hold power. Understanding prayers from God's Word and turning them into Scripture requests will ignite your prayer life.

As with the other devotionals in this series, we have divided this one into Old and New Testament references. You will discover the different Hebrew and Greek words for "prayer." Understanding the slight differences of "prayer" can bring greater meaning to what God is trying to teach.

God loves us and has given us His Word as a road map for life. It teaches everything needed to overcome life's obstacles. We must study and apply it for powerful living. Join us in equipping ourselves with *PrayerFULL: Your 30-Day Devotional to Ignite Biblical Prayer against Spiritual Warfare*.

Marta E Greenman   *Maureen H Maldonado*

INSTRUCTIONS

Thank you for choosing *PrayerFULL: Your 30-Day Devotional to Ignite Biblical Prayer against Spiritual Warfare.* This book has a specific purpose. Below we will explain how to best utilize it for your daily devotionals. Many people are unfamiliar with the Hebrew or Greek words. Do not allow them to intimidate you. You don't need to know how to pronounce the word to learn what it means.

The purpose of PrayerFULL is to learn to pray Scripture.

The daily plan is to focus on a prayer from God's Word.
- First, read the Scripture.
- Second, read the context to clarify the reference.
- Third, read the example prayer.
- Fourth, read the Scripture again and answer the questions.
- Finally, you will write you own prayer based on the Scripture.

After two days, you will be familiar with our procedure. This investment will be just ten to fifteen minutes a day. We believe your faithfulness in learning to pray God's Word will reap benefits for a lifetime.

Praying with you and for you,

Marta E Greenman *Maureen H Maldonado*

PrayerFULL

SECTION ONE
OLD TESTAMENT

Psalm 142:1-7 is our example of the Hebrew word zaʿaq.

"The basic meaning of this root is 'to cry for help in time of distress.'" It is used mainly in the Qal, but occurs a few times in the Niphal and Hiphil, where it carries distinctive meanings. It is parallel in meaning to *ṣāʿaq*. The two roots are doubtless mere variants, as is not unusual with such similar sibilants.

In the Qal stem, the word is used almost exclusively in reference to a cry from a disturbed heart, in need of some kind of help. The cry is not in summons of another, but an expression of the need felt. Most frequently, the cry is directed to God. When the Israelites were being invaded annually by the Midianites, they expressed this cry (Jud 6:6–7). Occasionally it is directed to a false deity (Jer 11:12), and once to a king (II Sam 19:29). A few times the word is used for a cry not directed to anyone, but simply as a note of alarm. All the city of Shiloh so cried out when told that the Ark had been captured by the Philistines (I Sam 4:13). The cry may be sounded in behalf of another person (Isa 15:5). It may be in lament at bad news (Jer 47:2); or it may be a cry of protest (Job 31:38). In only one instance is the idea of summons involved, and that is when Jephthah called for Ephraimites to assist him against the Ammonites (Jud 12:2). This is still a cry for help".

[1] Leon J. Wood, "570 זעק," ed. R. Laird Harris, Gleason L. Archer Jr., and Bruce K. Waltke, *Theological Wordbook of the Old Testament* (Chicago: Moody Press, 1999), 248.

OUR STORY
Pray About Everything!
Part 1

It has taken me a long life to learn that God really does answer our prayers, but not always in the way we would like. Sometimes He answers and grants our requests; occasionally He just says, "No", and at times He does it in His own way. When we moved to Texas, God did not answer my prayers as I wanted by granting me what I asked for but, came along and completely magnified what He was doing in my life.

Relocating is a challenge. I tried to accept the transfer from Arizona to Texas with grace. In our six years in Arizona, I had established a wonderful group of women in a weekly

Bible study. My gym was close to my home where my Bible study friends and I did our best to stay healthy. My life was happy and fulfilled, so I prayed God would provide similar situations in Texas.

Once in Texas, I learned God had His own plans! The study groups did not meet my needs at the time, and the gyms did not offer what I wanted.

The Lord did not immediately provide what I had requested, but He led me into something so much better. I was teaching at a local church (justmoved.org) for women who had relocated. Marta was the staff person assigned to oversee my performance since I was new to that church. I was intimidated by this godly woman who would be in my classes each week.

Fast forward twelve years. Marta is not only my dear friend, but I call her my personal Bible study teacher. I have been on her Bible study editing teams, we co-host a weekly radio show, and now God has us writing devotionals together. What joy this has brought to my life! I never could have imagined God would answer my prayer for a Bible study in this manner by actually putting me at the forefront of writing for Him. Oh, and God provided a small gym with Christian friends who support and encourage one another.

Dear friend, never doubt that God will answer your prayer. Be excited about what His answer will be!!! The promise of Ephesians 3:20 is for all His disciples, *"Now to Him who is able to do far more abundantly beyond all that we ask or think, according to the power that works within us."* Believe it! He is able.

Maureen H. Maldonado

OUR STORY
Pray About Everything!
Part 2

I moved to the Dallas area in 1993 when Marshall and I married. Everything was new; a new marriage, a new job, a new home; a new city and state! The first year seemed to pass quickly, but after the first year I found myself very lonely. This feeling was new for me. Growing up in a family of six, I dreamed of time alone. Living in the town of my childhood, I had friends since kindergarten. There was never a day I could not pick up the phone and have at least ten people to occupy my time.

One day I found myself weeping. I couldn't understand what was wrong since I was happy in my marriage, my job, and generally my life. What was I missing? I was missing a friend or a few friends to go with me through life. Proverbs 18:24 tells us, "*A person of many friends comes to ruin, but there is a friend who sticks closer than a brother.*" That was what I needed, so I began to pray for a friend to come into my life.

My prayer wasn't answered immediately or dramatically. But God has placed some of the finest people in my life these last 30 years that are "friends who stick closer than a brother."

Some don't even live in the United States! Some I speak with several times a week and some only a few times a year, but there is a bond only God can provide when He puts people together.

I met Maureen during a period of transition. God had returned us to the U.S. from seven years of service in Romania. Quite frankly, I was more than a little upset at God; I was downright mad. I couldn't understand why He moved us back to the States. I was His "yes girl." Isaiah 6:8-9a says, *"I heard the voice of the Lord, saying, 'Whom shall I send, and who will go for Us?' Then I said, 'Here am I. Send me!' And He said, 'Go, and tell this people…'"* This Scripture perfectly described me. I would have gone anywhere in the world for God.

Why would He be calling me back to America? The U.S. has more churches and more resources than any place in the world. I did not understand why He would want me here

when so many other places needed what I could offer. It didn't make sense; I was hurt and angry. I had no choice, God kept saying, "Trust Me." I'm convinced God has the best sense of humor. Many times God has reminded me, "See, I have this under control. I know what I'm doing."

Maureen didn't know much about the trials and tribulations in my life then, and at the time, I knew very little about her. But what has become of this God-ordained providential meeting was nothing less than a miracle. She has become a friend I get to do life with. We've laughed together, wept together, plotted and planned together, but most importantly we've prayed together. These days there is not a time we meet that we don't pray. I pray God answers your prayers by sending you a "Maureen" as He did mine. You will be blessed.

Marta E Greenman

DAY 1
PRAYER FOR HELP IN TIME OF TROUBLE

"I cry aloud with my voice to the LORD; I make supplication with my voice to the LORD.

2 I pour out my complaint before Him; I declare my trouble before Him. 3 When my spirit was overwhelmed within me, Thou didst know my path. In the way where I walk They have hidden a trap for me. 4 Look to the right and see; For there is no one who regards me; There is no escape for me; No one cares for my soul. 5 I cried out to Thee, O LORD; I said, "Thou art my refuge, My portion in the land of the living. 6 "Give heed to my cry, For I am brought very low; Deliver me from my persecutors, for they are too strong for me. 7 "Bring my soul out of prison, so that I may give thanks to Thy name; The righteous will surround me, For Thou wilt deal bountifully with me."

Psalm 142:1-7

CONTEXT

After David slew Goliath, 1 Samuel 18 tells us Saul was afraid of David, so he plotted against him. Saul knew the Lord had departed from him and was with David. After several murderous attempts on his life, David went into hiding in caves. Psalm 142 is a prayer of David crying out to the Lord during this time. 1 Samuel 22:1-2 describes the events surrounding David's prayer.

PRAYER

Father God, You are El Roi, the God who sees. Nothing takes You by surprise. I thank You that we can come to You with our problems that seem so small and finite when compared to Your grand creation. But You tell us to ask, Father. Matthew 7:7 teaches us, *"Ask and it shall be given to you. Seek and you shall find. Knock and it shall be opened to you."* Father, we are asking, we are seeking You, and we are trusting that You will answer.

My heart is heavy today because (speak your concern). You have seen my trouble, and my spirit is weighed down with burdens. You know and understand my pain. I feel as if I am alone in this battle and only You understand. There is no place to escape, and only You care for my soul. Though evil surrounds me, *"Blessed be the Lord, who daily bears our burden, the God who is our salvation,"* (Psalm 68:19).

Father, let us keep our eyes on You. Let us make You our refuge. You are our defender. As You told Moses and the children of Israel when Pharoah was pursuing them, the Lord will fight for you when you keep silent (Exodus 14:14). My responsibility is to cry out to You, to leave my burdens at Your feet, and to continue in Your plans for me.

Father, You are my portion, You are my deliverer. When the enemy is too strong, I know You are my redeemer. Therefore, I will continually give thanks to Your holy name. You are my righteousness. You will deal with my enemies, and I will forever praise Your name.

In the mighty name of Jesus.

Marta E Greenman *Maureen H Maldonado*

REFLECTION

Review Psalm 142:1-7

1. Was David comfortable making his request known to the Lord? List from scripture what proves your answer. (vv. 1-4)

   _____
   _____
   _____
   _____
   _____

2. What did the Lord do for David? (vv. 5-7)

   _____
   _____
   _____
   _____
   _____

3. Have you ever felt like everything was going against you? What do you learn from David's example?

   _____
   _____
   _____
   _____
   _____

PRAYER

Write your prayer for help in time of trouble:

Numbers 14:11-19 is our example for the Hebrew word nāʾ.

"Particle of entreaty or exhortation (e.g. Gen 12:13; Num 20:10). An interesting example of the use of this particle is found in Ps 118:25. hôšîʿâ nāʾ. "O Lord save us" (NIV). This cry was taken up at the time of the triumphal entry when the crowd quoted the context also "blessed is he who comes in the name of the Lord (v. 26; Mt 21:9). The Greek hōsanna is a transliteration of the Hebrew phrase "O save us," even including the phonetic doubling of the n of the particle nāʾ. In Lk 19:39 it is recorded that some of the Pharisees called on Jesus to rebuke his disciples for this outburst, but he instead declared that if the disciples were quiet the very stones would speak. One reason for the Pharisees' reaction, doubtless, is that in the OT the cry "save us" is addressed to the Lord (YHWH). In the NT it is addressed to Jesus, the Son of David. The Pharisees regarded this ascription of praise to Jesus as high blasphemy, though they ascribed it to the ignorance of the crowds. Jesus accepted it as glorious truth."

[2] *R. Laird Harris, "1269 אן," ed. R. Laird Harris, Gleason L. Archer Jr., and Bruce K. Waltke, Theological Wordbook of the Old Testament (Chicago: Moody Press, 1999), 541.*

DAY 2
PRAYER FOR THE REBELLIOUS

"*11 And the LORD said to Moses, 'How long will this people spurn Me? And how long will they not believe in Me, despite all the signs which I have performed in their midst? 12 I will smite them with pestilence and dispossess them, and I will make you into a nation greater and mightier than they.' 13 But Moses said to the LORD, 'Then the Egyptians will hear of it, for by Thy strength Thou didst bring up this people from their midst, 14 and they will tell it to the inhabitants of this land. They have heard that Thou, O LORD, art in the midst of this people, for Thou, O LORD, art seen eye to eye, while Thy cloud stands over them; and Thou dost go before them in a pillar of cloud by day and in a pillar of fire by night. 15 Now if Thou dost slay this people as one man, then the nations who have heard of Thy fame will say, 16 'Because the LORD could not bring this people into the land which He promised them by oath, therefore He slaughtered them in the wilderness.' 17 But now, I pray, let the power of the Lord be great, just as Thou hast declared, 18 The LORD is slow to anger and abundant in lovingkindness, forgiving iniquity and transgression; but He will by no means clear the guilty, visiting the iniquity of the fathers on the children to the third and the fourth generations. 19 'Pardon, I pray, the iniquity of this people according to the greatness of Thy lovingkindness, just as Thou also hast forgiven this people, from Egypt even until now.'"*

Numbers 14:11-19

CONTEXT

Moses, at the command of the Lord, sent 12 spies into Canaan to bring back a report before they were to cross into the promised land. Ten spies brought back a bad report, saying the people of the land were too strong, the cities were fortified, and the descendants of Anak were there (Numbers 13:28). Only Joshua and Caleb believed the Lord and said, *"We should take possession of the Land,"* (Numbers 13:30). The children of Israel cried out and grumbled against Moses and Aaron saying, *"Why is the Lord bringing us into the land to fall by the sword, let us appoint a leader and return to Egypt,"* (Numbers 14:3-4). Moses pleaded with the congregation to not rebel against the Lord and to not fear the people of the land. But the congregation said, *"Stone them,"* (Numbers 14:9-10). The Lord questioned Moses about the Jews not believing in Him despite all the signs He had performed for them. *"I will smite them and make you a nation greater and mightier than they."* (Numbers 14:11-12). Then Moses began to pray.

PRAYER

Father, Moses teaches us to pray for those who are rebellious and grumbling against You, ungrateful and undeserving of Your love. We, like Moses, want to remind You, You are great, You are slow to anger, and abundant in lovingkindness. You forgive transgressions, but by no means do You clear the guilty. As Moses pleaded on behalf of Israel so the Egyptians could not point the finger at You, I am praying for _____. Lord do not let them say You abandoned Your people and slaughtered them in the wilderness (Numbers 14:16).

Father, remind me to pray as Moses prayed. I think of our nation. The U.S. was founded on Biblical principles by our founding fathers who believed in You. We have strayed so far from You. We have sinned against You and have replaced You with idols of all types. We have made a god in our own

image. We have sacrificed children on the altar of Molech and called it freedom of choice. We have forsaken the Biblical tenants of marriage in the approval of adultery, same sex marriage, and any sexual sin outside the bounds of Biblical marriage. We have removed prayer from school, from the legal system, and from all government functions.

Even when America deserves judgment, we must pray for mercy. Internationally, people still think we are a godly nation. Therefore, I pray You pardon the iniquities of America - not because we deserve it, but so the other nations would see America is still aligned with You. Father, raise up righteous people to take hold of every aspect of our country, including but not limited to government, businesses, homes, schools, hospitals, etc. You are the God of Abraham, Isaac, and Jacob, the true and living God. Let us repent and serve You alone.

In the mighty name of Jesus.

Marta E Greenman   *Maureen H Maldonado*

41

REFLECTION

Review Numbers 14:13-19.

1. Why was Moses pleading for the children of Israel when they didn't deserve it? (Numbers 14:13)

   _____
   _____
   _____

2. Which characteristic did Moses remind the Lord about Himself? (Numbers 14:18)

   _____
   _____
   _____

3. What request did Moses ask on behalf of the children of Israel? (Numbers 14:19)

   _____
   _____
   _____

4. Whom do you need to pray for who are like the Israelites? (grumblers, non-deserving)

   _____
   _____
   _____
   _____
   _____

PRAYER

Write your prayer for help in time of trouble:

1 Chronicles 4:10 is our example for the Hebrew word qārā'.

"The root *qr'* denotes primarily the enunciation of a specific vocable or message. In the case of the latter usage it is customarily addressed to a specific recipient and is intended to elicit a specific response (hence, it may be translated "proclaim, invite"). Infrequently, *qārā'* denotes just an outcry (e.g. Ps 147:9; Isa 34:14). Our root with the same semantic distribution occurs in Old Aramaic (KAI, II, p. 41), Canaanite (H. Donner and W. Rollig, KAI, Il, p. 22), and Ugaritic (UT 19: no. 2267). The most frequently recurring synonyms are *ṣ/zaʿaq*, *šāwaʿ* (to cry out urgently for help, Jer 20:8). The root occurs 689 times.

The verb may represent the specification of a name. Naming is sometimes an assertion of sovereignty over the thing named. God's creating entailed naming and numbering the stars (Ps 147:4), the darkness (Gen 1:5), indeed all things (Isa 40:26). God presented the animals to Adam to assert his relative sovereignty over them (Gen 2:19). God sovereignly called Cyrus by name (note that election to a task is involved here, Isa 45:4). Sometimes this idea of sovereignty is entailed even though the concept "naming" is omitted, e.g., God called all generations from the beginning (Isa 41:4; cf. Amos 5:8)."

---

⁵ Leonard J. Coppes, "2063 אָרָק," ed. R. Laird Harris, Gleason L. Archer Jr., and Bruce K. Waltke, *Theological Wordbook of the Old Testament* (Chicago: Moody Press, 1999), 810.

DAY 3
PRAYER OF JABEZ

"⁰ Now Jabez called on the God of Israel, saying, 'Oh that Thou wouldst bless me indeed, and enlarge my border, and that Thy hand might be with me, and that Thou wouldst keep me from harm, that it may not pain me!' And God granted him what he requested."

1 Chronicles 4:10

CONTEXT

The books of First and Second Chronicles follow the history of the people of Israel from Adam - approximately 4,000 BC - to the fall of Jerusalem, and until the Jews returned during the reign of Cyrus, the Persian king in 539 BC. God's chosen people had been sent into exile in Babylon for 70 years until God turned the heart of King Cyrus who allowed Israel to return to Jerusalem from exile and rebuild the temple.

Because the Jews did not want to forget all God had done for them, nor those who had come before them, they recorded their history. Chronicles was written as a genealogy of God's chosen people. Jabez' name is tucked into 1 Chronicles 4. Jabez was a descendent of Judah, one of the twelve tribes of Israel. Jesus is also from the tribe of Judah.

In Biblical times a name was an important part of one's identity and often has historical significance. There were times when one had to overcome the name or change the name. God changed Abram's name to Abraham, Sari's name to Sarah, and Jacob's name to Israel to align their names with the new course trajectory of their lives and futures.

Jabez' mother bore him in pain, thus the reason for his name. ("Jabez" translates as "he makes sorrowful.") Jabez did not want to accept that his life was sad or sorrowful, so he prayed for God's divine intervention. Scripture tells us Jabez was more honorable than his brothers, and God honored his request.

PRAYER

Dear Lord, we come to You as humble servants overcome with the goodness You bestow on our daily lives. Let us echo the words of Jabez as we pray, *"Oh that Thou wouldst bless me indeed, and enlarge my border, and that Thy hand might be with me, and that Thou wouldst keep me from harm"* (1 Chronicles 4:10).

Like Jabez, many are born into a difficult life, surrounded by poverty and hardships. His was a time when people did whatever pleased them, which sounds so much like our world today.

Lord, I pray as Jabez that You would bless me indeed. Blessings come from YOU, and no one else. This does not mean I want more possessions, but I want a closer relationship with You. Lord, in John 16:24, You said, *"Until now you have asked for nothing in My name; ask, and you will receive, that your joy may be made full."* I am asking. Therefore, I will wait with great expectation.

Lord, I also ask You to enlarge my territory solely on Your plan for my life. Again, I am not asking for more real estate, but through my words and actions I bring more people to You and to Your Word. Like Jabez, I want to impact Your kingdom. Please help me to reclaim territory for the kingdom that Satan has stolen and be a light to people who are easily influenced by the darkness of this world. Father God, I ask You to keep Your hand upon me. In Psalm 63:8 we are told, *"Thy right hand upholds me."* I request Your presence be with me every moment of every day. I ask that You guide me through circumstances and trials that come my way. Please cover me with Your hands of love, care, and protection. Please use me as Your hands to hold and heal others as they search for You.

Finally, God, please protect me from harm so I may be free from pain. Lord, I need Your peace and protection from temptation and harm. I pray, Lord, You will grant my request.

In the mighty name of Jesus.

Marta E Greenman   *Maureen H Maldonado*

REFLECTION

Review 1 Chronicles 4:10.

1. Explain why your parents chose your name.

   _____
   _____
   _____

2. What does your name mean?

   _____
   _____
   _____

3. Give examples of how you are living up to the meaning of your name or changing your life because of it.

   _____
   _____
   _____
   _____
   _____
   _____
   _____
   _____

PRAYER

Write your own personal prayer of Jabez:

"The prayer of _____ (insert your name)".

_____
_____
_____
_____
_____
_____
_____
_____
_____
_____
_____
_____
_____
_____
_____
_____
_____
_____

In this devotional we have five Scriptures that use our Hebrew word Pālal, they are: 1 Samuel 1:10-11; 1 Samuel 2:1-10; 2 Kings 20:2-3; Nehemiah 1:4-11; and Jonah 2:1-9.

"The verb is found eighty-four times in the OT [OLD TESTAMENT], usually in the Hithpael (except Gen 48:11; I Sam 2:25; Ps 106:30; Ezk 16:52). The usual translation for the root in the Hithpael is "to pray." The semantic development behind this will be discussed below.

There is a rich nomenclature for "praying" in the OT. There are at least a dozen Hebrew words for pray and prayer. But easily the most common word for "prayer" is tĕpillâ and the related verb, pālal. A number of suggestions have been made for the etymology of pālal. Wellhausen in the 19th century connected it with the Arabic falla, "to notch the edge of a sword" and thus pālal, it was thought, meant "to cut or wound oneself," and reflected the pagan custom of slashing oneself in a frenzy during worship, a practice forbidden by the law (Deut 14:1)."

[4] Victor P. Hamilton, "1776 פלל," ed. R. Laird Harris, Gleason L. Archer Jr., and Bruce K. Waltke, *Theological Wordbook of the Old Testament* (Chicago: Moody Press, 1999), 725.

DAY 4
PRAYER OF THE AFFLICTED

"¹⁰ She [Hannah], greatly distressed, prayed to the LORD and wept bitterly. ¹¹ And she made a vow and said, "LORD of hosts, if Thou will indeed look on the affliction of Thy maidservant and remember me, and not forget Thy maidservant, but will give Thy maidservant a son, then I will give him to the LORD all the days of his life, and a razor shall never come on his head."

1 Samuel 1:10-11

CONTEXT

Elkanah had two wives, Hannah and Peninnah. Peninnah had children and Hannah was childless. Peninnah provoked Hannah bitterly and irritated her because she was barren. Because of this, Elkanah would give Hannah a double portion because he loved her so. Elkanah asked, *"Hannah, why do you weep and why do you not eat and why is your heart sad? Am I not better to you than ten sons?"* (1 Samuel 1:8). Hannah then went to the temple and in great distress prayed to the Lord.

PRAYER

Father, thank You that we can run to You in our affliction and know You will hear our pleas, especially when we cry. Even when those around us misunderstand, ignore, or misconstrue our dilemma, You are always there. At times people taunt us which compounds our pain, but let us be persistent in our prayers and find comfort in You.

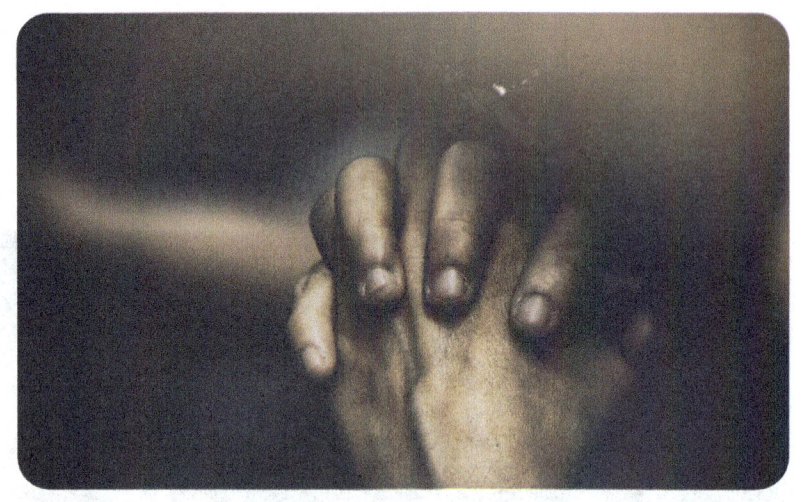

2 Corinthians 1:4 teaches, *"Who comforts us in all our affliction so that we may be able to comfort those who are in any affliction with the comfort with which we ourselves are comforted by God."* Father, we thank You that You are the source of our comfort. We thank You that your Scripture tells us we will be able to be a source of comfort for others. You will use our pain for Your glory. Therefore, let us be diligent to do whatever is necessary to become whole and healthy in You.

Father, let us be persistent in our prayers. You tell us in Matthew 7:7-8, *"Ask, and it shall be given to you; seek, and you shall find; knock, and it shall be opened. For everyone who asks receives, and he who seeks finds, and to him who knocks it shall be opened."* Let us pray until our doors are opened.

Let us be thankful Your will is the right will. You only do what is best for us and it is so difficult when we are desperate for the answer. Help us trust Your will is perfect.

Just like Hannah, when she left the temple, we want to rejoice in You, even when we do not have the answer we are searching. We cannot allow our circumstances to steal our joy. Proverbs 4:23 tells us," *Watch over your heart with all diligence, for from it flow the springs of life."* No matter what is happening in our lives and in the world, help us find joy in spending time in Your word and in Your presence.

In the mighty name of Jesus.

Marta E Greenman   *Maureen H Maldonado*

REFLECTION

Review 1 Samuel 1:1-20

1. What did the priest believe about Hannah? (v. 13)

   _____
   _____
   _____

2. How did Hannah respond to the priest? (vv. 15-16)

   _____
   _____
   _____

3. When Hannah left the temple, Scripture says, "her face was no longer sad." Yet, she did not know if the Lord would grant her prayer and give her a child. What can we learn from this?

   _____
   _____
   _____
   _____
   _____
   _____
   _____

PRAYER

Write your prayer for the afflicted:

DAY 5
PRAYER OF REJOICING

"*¹Then Hannah prayed and said, "My heart exults in the LORD; My horn is exalted in the LORD, My mouth speaks boldly against my enemies, Because I rejoice in Thy salvation. ² "There is no one holy like the LORD, indeed, there is no one besides Thee, nor is there any rock like our God. ³ "Boast no more so very proudly, do not let arrogance come out of your mouth; For the LORD is a God of knowledge, And with Him actions are weighed. ⁴ "The bows of the mighty are shattered, But the feeble gird on strength. ⁵ "Those who were full hire themselves out for bread, but those who were hungry cease to hunger. Even the barren gives birth to seven, but she who has many children languishes. ⁶ "The LORD kills and makes alive; He brings down to Sheol and raises up.*

⁷ "The LORD makes poor and rich; He brings low, He also exalts. ⁸ "He raises the poor from the dust, He lifts the needy from the ash heap to make them sit with nobles, And inherit a seat of honor; For the pillars of the earth are the LORD's, And He set the world on them. ⁹ "He keeps the feet of His godly ones, But the wicked ones are silenced in darkness; For not by might shall a man prevail. ¹⁰ "Those who contend with the LORD will be shattered; Against them He will thunder in the heavens, The LORD will judge the ends of the earth; and He will give strength to His king, and will exalt the horn of His anointed.'"

1 Samuel 2:1-10

CONTEXT

Hannah had gone to the temple and pleaded with the Lord concerning her mistreatment and her infertility. As she left the temple without knowing the answer the Lord would bestow, she returned home *"no longer sad."* The Lord answered her prayer by blessing her with a son whom she named Samuel. His name means, *"I have asked him of the Lord."* 1 Samuel 2:1-10 is Hannah's prayer of thanksgiving.

PRAYER

Father, we exalt You that You are God and You are a God who answers prayer. You are a God of miracles, and we are thankful that there is no one like You. You are our hope, our life, and our salvation is in You.

Father, if we are to boast, let us boast in You, not in our own accomplishments. Everything we have is from You, through You, and for Your glory. Let us not be arrogant, but humble. "(Let) *not one of you be puffed up, for one against another"* (1 Corinthians 4:6b KJV). Lord, You are the God of knowledge. We trust You to weigh our actions and the actions of others who have harmed us.

We thank You that You have given heed to our prayer. Let us shout to the ends of the earth Your praise. Let us make Your name known to all the nations for You are God and greatly to be praised. You have heard the prayers of the meek and lowly and You answered them just as You answered the prayers of kings. We are equal in Your eyes. Galatians 3:28 tells us, *"There is neither Jew nor Greek, there is neither slave nor free man, there is neither male nor female; for you are all one in Christ Jesus."*

Let us remember how significant we are in Your eyes, even when those around us may not notice us. You tell us in Psalm 139 that You ordained our days, and we are fearfully and wonderfully made.

Father, we thank You when those who come against us are judged rightly. You are our defender and are the defender of the innocent. Let us always put our trust in You. You tell us if our enemy is hungry, we are to feed him, or if thirsty to give him drink. For we know, *"vengeance is mine, I will repay, saith the Lord,"* (Romans 12:19-20). Let us not overcome evil with evil, but overcome evil with good (Romans 12:21).

In the mighty name of Jesus.

Marta E Greenman *Maureen H Maldonado*

REFLECTION

Review 1 Samuel 2:1-10

1. What does 1 Samuel say about boasting? (v. 3)
   - _____
   - _____

2. What does the Lord do? (vv. 6-7)
   - _____
   - _____
   - _____
   - _____
   - _____
   - _____
   - _____
   - _____

3. Where will the Lord judge? (v. 10)

   _____
   _____
   _____
   _____
   _____
   _____

PRAYER

Write your prayer of rejoicing:

MY STORY
Answered Prayer

Several years ago, Marta, three other women, and I travelled to a Muslim country. One of the women was Marta's 85 years young mom, Lillie, full of life and excitement for living.

We had been "working" for Jesus several days, holding seminars, prayer nights, and meetings. We took a day off to shop and see the sights. Did I say shop? You see, shopping is one of my favorite things to do, and Lillie has the gift of shopping also! The day was warm, but we were not put off by the heat and were excited to see what treasures awaited us.

Marta did not join us that day since she was meeting with church leaders, so I was in charge of making sure all went well on our shopping expedition. We began the day by taking a leisurely hike straight up a mountain pass. Remember, Lillie was 85, so the hike was definitely a stretch for her, but she was very happy to get out and see the sights. Our next stop was in the downtown area at a street fair. There were more than a hundred booths for shoppers to browse and buy, and we did our share of contributing to the local economy.

We were tired and it was getting extremely hot when suddenly I noticed Lillie was not looking well. We searched for and quickly found shade (thank You, Lord) and water. But Lillie was fading fast. I thought she was showing all the signs of heat stroke and appeared to be in a medically dangerous state. We applied wet towels all over her. We quickly turned to prayer. I was so afraid I would have to tell Marta I had taken her mother shopping, and she didn't make it!

We prayed nonstop, taking turns asking God to save Lillie. Eventually, we saw our dear sweet Lillie beginning to revive. We offered thanks and praise to God! We knew she was going to be alright! About this time Marta arrived. What a story we had to tell about the amazing way God had answered our prayers and kept her momma alive and well.

In my heart, I believe we almost lost Lillie that day. Never doubt God and never stop praying!

Maureen H Maldonado

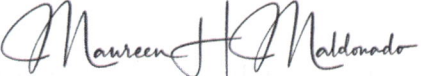

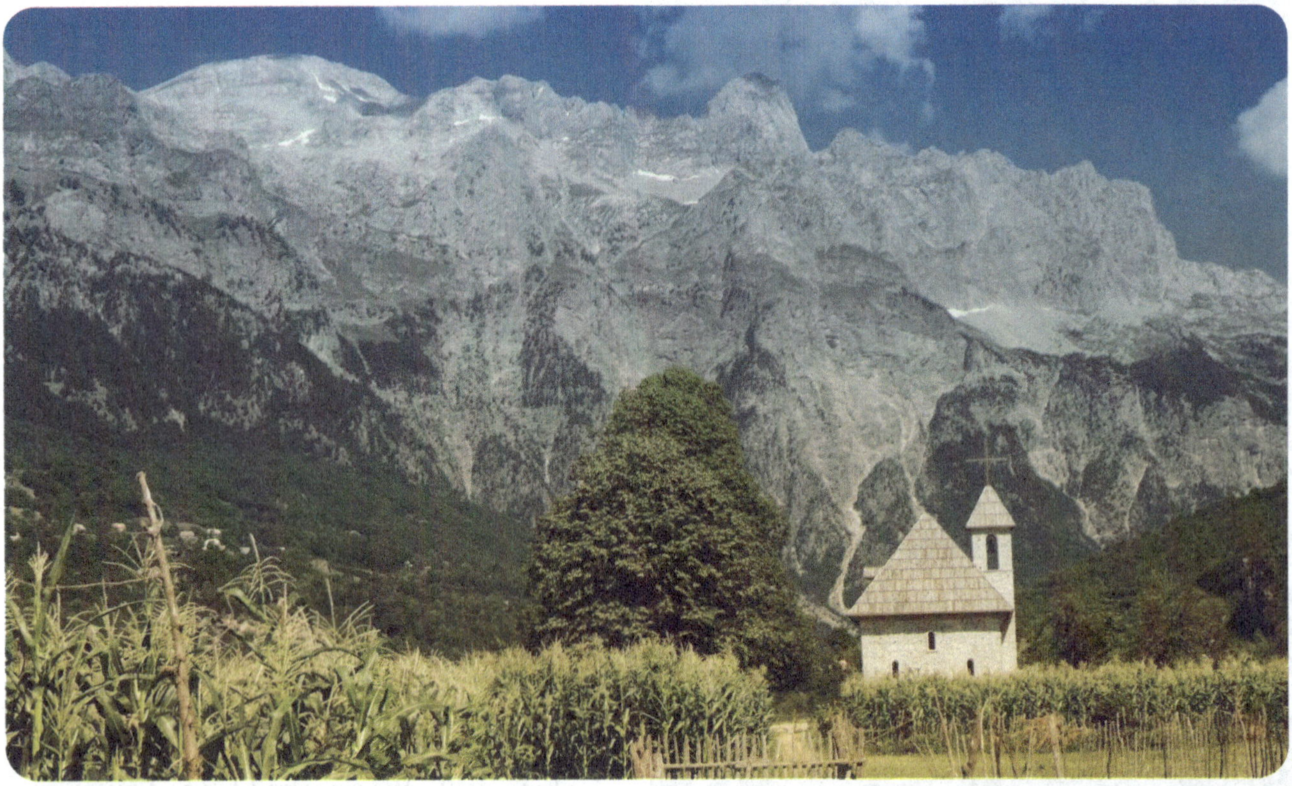

DAY 6
PRAYER FOR PHYSICAL HEALING

"In those days Hezekiah became mortally ill. And Isaiah the prophet, the son of Amoz, came to him and said to him, Thus says the LORD says: 'Set your house in order, for you shall die and not live.' ² Then he turned his face to the wall and prayed to the LORD, saying, ³ 'Remember now O LORD, I beseech Thee how I have walked before Thee in truth and with a whole heart, and have done what is good in Thy sight!' And Hezekiah wept bitterly. ⁴ And it came about before Isaiah had gone out of the middle court, that the word of the LORD came to him, saying, ⁵ Return and say to Hezekiah the leader of My people, Thus says the LORD, the God of your father David: 'I have heard your prayer, I have seen your tears; behold, I will heal you. On the third day you shall go up to the house of the LORD. ⁶ And 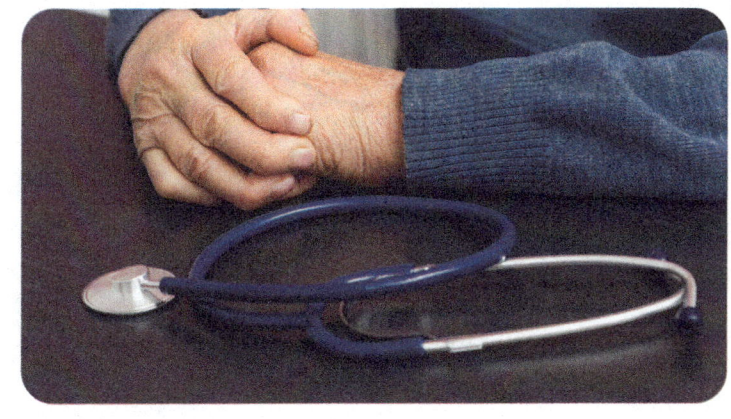 I will add fifteen years to your life, and I will deliver you and this city from the hand of the king of Assyria; and I will defend this city for My own sake and for My servant David's sake.' ⁷ Then Isaiah said, 'Take a cake of figs.' And they took and laid it on the boil, and he recovered. ⁸ Now Hezekiah said to Isaiah, 'What will be the sign that the LORD will heal me, and that I will go up to the house of the LORD the third day?' ⁹ And Isaiah said, 'This shall be the sign to you from the LORD, that the LORD will do the thing that He has spoken: shall the shadow go forward ten steps or go back ten steps?'" ¹⁰ So Hezekiah answered, 'It is easy for the shadow to decline ten steps; no, but let the shadow turn backward ten steps.' ¹¹ And Isaiah the prophet cried to the LORD, and He brought the shadow on the stairway back ten steps by which it had gone down on the stairway of Ahaz."

2 Kings 20:1-11

CONTEXT

King Hezekiah was 25 years old when he became king of the Southern kingdom, Judah, from 728 B.C. to 686 B.C. He trusted the Lord and removed the high places (places of pagan worship). After him, there was none like him. He clung to the Lord and did not depart from following Him. The Lord was with him. Hezekiah rebelled against the king of Assyria and defeated the Philistines at the Gaza strip. (2 Kings 18:1-8)

In 701 B.C., Hezekiah prayed to the Lord to heal him from his mortal illness. The Lord saw his tears, heard his cry, and answered his prayer.

PRAYER

Father God, You are the same yesterday, today and forever. You are the God who healed in ancient times, You are the God who heals today. Only You have the power to give life, take away life, extend life, or shorten life.

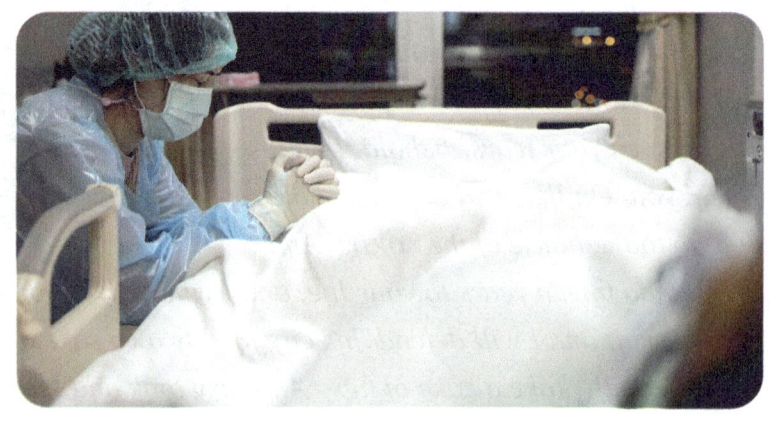

You are Jehovah Rapha, the God Who heals. Psalm 103:3 teaches, *"Who pardons your iniquities and heals all your diseases."* May we always come to You first with our requests. May we rely on You as our deliverer and not man.

Father, I pray now for the healing of (insert name). Just as you added years of life to King Hezekiah, add years of life to (insert name). Just as King Hezekiah, *"walked before Thee in truth and with a whole heart, and have done what is good in Thy sight."* (2 Kings 20:3) Heal (insert name) completely in spirit, soul, and body. Father, You honored Hezekiah, please do the same with (insert name).

Help us in our time of weakness, sustain us, strengthen us, show us Your power, and show us Your glory. There was no sickness before sin. Jesus, You gave us victory by Your death on the cross. We eagerly await Your return and spending eternity with You where there will be no sickness or pain.

Father, let us never forget to give You praise when we receive Your gracious healing whether you heal us on earth or the ultimate healing of spending eternity with You in heaven. Let us be like the apostle Paul who said, "*To live is Christ, to die is gain*" (Philippians 1:21). Let us be hard pressed in both directions, having the desire to depart and be with Christ, but understanding that it is necessary for the sake of the church to remain (Philippians 1:23-24). We give You all the praise, honor, and glory.

In the mighty name of Jesus.

Marta E Greenman *Maureen H Maldonado*

REFLECTION

Review 2 Kings 20:1-11

1. What did the Lord tell King Hezekiah was going to happen? (v. 1)

   _____

   _____

2. What was Hezekiah's prayer to the Lord? (For what was he praying?) (v. 3)

   _____

   _____

3. The word of the Lord came to Isaiah…(Fill in the blanks below) (vv. 5-6)

   The Lord:

   _____ your prayer

   _____ your tears

   _____ you

   Result: What did the Lord say would happen on the third day?

   _____ 15 years to your life,

   _____ you and this city from the hand of the king of Assyria,

   _____ defend the city for My own sake.

4. The Lord said He would bring a sign to show that He answered the prayer. The sign was to have the shadow go back ten steps. What does verse 11 tell us about how the Lord answered the king's prayer?

   _____

   _____

PRAYER

Write your prayer of physical healing for _____:

_____
_____
_____
_____
_____
_____
_____
_____
_____
_____
_____
_____
_____
_____
_____
_____
_____
_____
_____

DAY 7
PRAYER OF DISTRESS

"⁴ Now when I heard these words, I sat down and wept and mourned for days; and I was fasting and praying before the God of heaven. ⁵ And I said, "I beseech Thee, O LORD God of heaven, the great and awesome God, who preserves the covenant and lovingkindness for those who love Him and keep His commandments: ⁶ Let Thine ear now be attentive and Thine eyes open, to hear the prayer of Thy servant which I am praying before Thee now, day and night, on behalf of the sons of Israel Thy servants, confessing the sins of the sons of Israel which we have committed against Thee; I and my father's house have sinned. ⁷ We have acted very corruptly against Thee and have not kept the commandments, nor the statutes, nor the ordinances which Thou didst command Thy servant Moses. ⁸ Remember the word which You command Thy servant Moses, saying, 'If you are unfaithful, I will scatter you among the peoples; ⁹ but if you return to Me and keep My commandments and do them, though those of you who have been scattered were in the most remote part of the heavens, I will gather them from there and bring them to the place where I have chosen to have My name dwell.' ¹⁰ And they are Thy servants and Thy people whom Thou didst redeem by Thy great power and by Thy strong hand. ¹¹ O Lord, I beseech Thee may Thine ear be attentive to the prayer of Thy servant and the prayer of Thy servants who delight to revere Thy name, and make Thy servant successful today and grant him mercy before this man."

Nehemiah 1:4-11

CONTEXT

It is important to understand the distress of the children of Israel during that time. Nehemiah was weeping because of the destruction of the previous 150 years to the beautiful city of Jerusalem, to his people, and to the future.

Nehemiah is the last historical book of the Old Testament before the 400 silent years between the Old and New Testaments. King Nebuchadnezzar had captured Jerusalem in 605 B.C. Daniel and his friends were taken captive which began the 70 years of captivity mentioned in Daniel 9:24-27. By the time the Book of Nehemiah was written, only the poorest people (the remnant) remained in Jerusalem.

The Israelites, God's chosen people, had been in captivity for 70 years and had tried to rebuild the temple under great oppression. Haman had tried to annihilate the entire Jewish population as told in the Book of Esther. Nehemiah was weeping before the Lord because of all that had happened. Israel had no protection on its borders.

PRAYER

Father God, we thank You for the prayers in Your Word that teach us how to pray for Your children, for nations, and for the lost. Today we come to You on behalf of (insert your country). You are the God who sees. You have seen our sins which are heaped like stacks of stones.

Just like Nehemiah, *"…we beseech You, Lord of heaven, the great and awesome God, who preserves the covenant and lovingkindness for those who love Him and keep His commandments"* (Nehemiah 1:5).

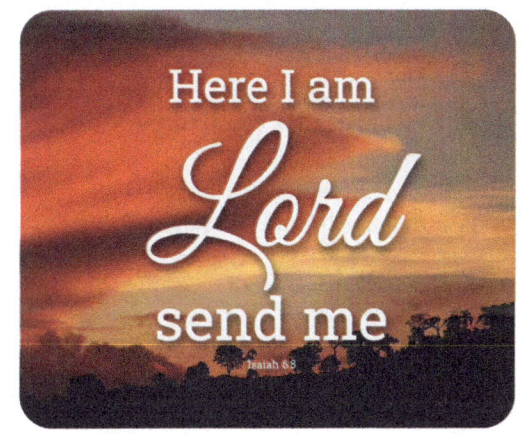

You tell us if we confess our sins You are faithful and will forgive them. 1 John 1:9-10 tells, *"If we confess our sins, He is faithful and righteous to forgive us our sins and to cleanse us from all unrighteousness. If we say that we have not sinned, we make Him a liar, and His word is not in us."* Father, let us turn to You, repent, humble ourselves, pray and seek Your face, and turn from our wicked ways. Then, You promised us, You would hear from heaven, forgive our sins and heal our land (2 Chronicles 7:14).

Let us be like Ezra, Esther, and Nehemiah. Once they prayed, they were called to action. Let us be diligent to hear what You, Father God, are telling us and be obedient to do what

You instruct. Let us be like Isaiah when he said, *"Here I am Lord, send me"* (Isaiah 6:8). Your Word tells us You will always have a remnant. Even though we may be small, Lord, let us be mighty.

Father, You are our salvation, our Deliverer, our Sustainer. In You we place our trust. Without You we are nothing. Please give us strength to stand in the gap and pray like Nehemiah for our country and for our world.

Marta E Greenman   *Maureen H Maldonado*

REFLECTION

Review Nehemiah 1: 1-11

1. What was the state of Jerusalem? (v. 3)

    The people?

    The city?

2. What did Nehemiah do when he heard the report about Jerusalem? (v. 4)

    _____

    _____

3. In verse 5, Nehemiah began his prayer with praise and adoration. Write the different attributes Nehemiah spoke about the Lord.

    - _____

    - _____

    - _____

4. What did Nehemiah specifically ask? (v. 6)

    _____

5. What did Nehemiah confess? (v. 7)

    _____

6. In verses 8-10 Nehemiah told the Lord he understood His people were in captivity because of their sins and he reminded the Lord of His promises. What was Nehemiah's request of the Lord in verse 11?

    _____

    _____

    _____

PRAYER

Write your prayer of distress:

_____
_____
_____
_____
_____
_____
_____
_____
_____
_____
_____
_____
_____
_____
_____
_____
_____
_____
_____
_____
_____

DAY 8
PRAYER OF THE REBELLIOUS - PART 1

"Then Jonah prayed to the LORD his God from the stomach of the fish, ² and he said, "I called out of my distress to the LORD, and He answered me. I cried for help from the depth of Sheol; Thou didst hear my voice. ³ For Thou hast cast me into the deep, into the heart of the seas, and the current engulfed me. All Thy breakers and billows passed over me. ⁴ So I said, 'I have been expelled from Thy sight. Nevertheless I will look again toward Thy holy temple.' ⁵ Water encompassed me to the point of death. The great deep engulfed me, weeds were wrapped around my head. ⁶ I descended to the roots of the mountains. The earth with its bars was around me forever, but Thou hast brought up my life from the pit, O LORD my God. ⁷ While I was fainting away, I remembered the LORD, and my prayer came to Thee, into Thy holy temple. ⁸ Those who regard vain idols forsake their faithfulness, ⁹ But I will sacrifice to Thee with the voice of thanksgiving. That which I have vowed I will pay. Salvation is from the LORD." ¹⁰Then the Lord commanded the fish, and it vomited Jonah up onto the dry land."

Jonah 2:1-10

CONTEXT

The Lord commanded Jonah to go to Nineveh, a town of pagans worshipping false gods, not a place Jonah wanted to visit. Instead of being obedient, Jonah ran in the opposite direction. As with all correction, the Lord's heart is to 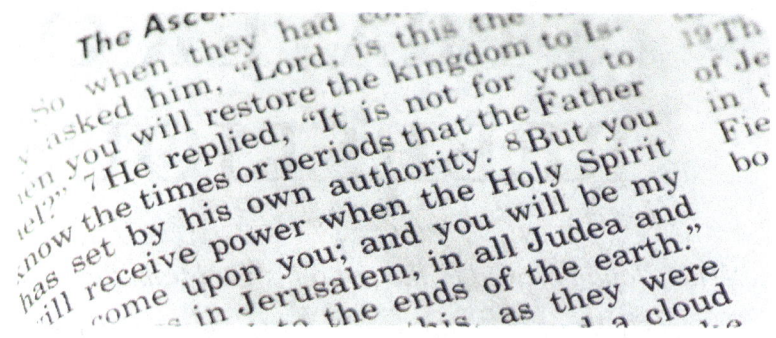 have a relationship with us and for His people to return to Him. When Jonah ran in disobedience, he was running away from the Lord, not from Nineveh. As a result, Jonah caused a crisis not only in his life, but in the innocent lives of his traveling companions. The Lord created a great storm which resulted in Jonah sacrificing himself to save the others on the ship. Instead of allowing Jonah to die, however, the Lord appointed a great fish to swallow him. Being swallowed by the whale was the Lord's correction to have Jonah rethink his opposition to the Lord's instruction to go to Nineveh.

PRAYER

Father, give me a heart for the lost, just like You. Let me not be like Jonah wishing calamity on them instead of repentance and forgiveness. Let me have a heart of obedience, a heart not to quarrel with You or grumble and complain. *"The name of the Lord is a strong tower; the righteous runs into it and is safe"* (Proverbs 18:10). Help me run to You, Lord, instead of running away from You.

Father, Your desire for Nineveh is much like our desire for our own country. Isaiah 55:5 states, *"Behold, you will call a nation you do not know, and a nation which knows you not will run to you, because of the Lord your God, even the Holy One of Israel; For He has glorified you."* Just

as the Lord wanted Jonah to be a witness to Nineveh, because of their great "wickedness," the Lord's heart was for Nineveh to repent and return to Him. That was the Lord's heart in Biblical times, and that is His heart today. Father let me have a heart like Yours that longs for people to know You and Your salvation. Let me always be willing to stand and proclaim Your name to those who need to hear Your message.

Just as You called Your disciples to be Your witnesses, let us be Your witnesses not only in our own country, but around the world. Let us live as the disciples did when the Lord commanded them in Acts 1:8, *"But you will receive power when the Holy Spirit has come upon you and you shall be my witness both in Jerusalem and in all Judea and Samaria and even the remotest parts of the earth."* Obedience is always a blessing, not only to myself but to those around me. If we do stray, pull us back quickly so we can return and have sweet fellowship with You.

In the mighty name of Jesus.

Marta E Greenman *Maureen H Maldonado*

REFLECTION

Review Jonah chapters 1 & 2

1. Why did God want Jonah to go to Nineveh? (Jonah 1:2)

   _____
   _____
   _____

2. What was Jonah's response? (Jonah 1:3)

   _____
   _____
   _____

3. What conclusion did the shipmates believe about the reason for the raging storm? (Jonah 1:10)

   _____
   _____
   _____

4. What did the shipmates do to Jonah and what was the result of their action? (Jonah 1:15-17)

   _____
   _____
   _____
   _____
   _____

PRAYER

Write your prayer for help in time of trouble:

DAY 9
PRAYER OF THE REBELLIOUS - PART 2

"² Then he prayed to the LORD and said, 'Please LORD, was this not what I said when I was still in my own country? Therefore, in order to forestall this I fled to Tarshish, for I knew that Thou art a gracious and compassionate God, slow to anger and abundant in lovingkindness, and one who relents concerning calamity. ³ Therefore now, O LORD, please take my life from me, for death is better to me than life.'"

Jonah 4:2-3

CONTEXT

Jonah was saved from the belly of the whale and went to Nineveh to proclaim the Lord's message. Jonah 3:3 tells us, *"So Jonah arose and went to Nineveh according to the word of the Lord. Now Nineveh was an exceedingly great city, a three days walk."* Jonah proclaimed the city would be overthrown unless the people repented. The king issued a proclamation for fasting, sackcloth, and ashes, calling for the city to turn from their wicked ways. Nineveh repented and the Lord did not bring calamity upon the city. Jonah, however, was angry that the Lord spared Nineveh.

PRAYER

Father, let us be like Jonah to know Your character and understand the words that Peter wrote in 2 Peter 3:9, *"The Lord is not slow about His promise, as some count slowness, but is patient towards you, not wishing for any to perish but for all to come to repentance."* But let us NOT be angry when You show compassion to those whom we believe are undeserving. Let us remember that, we too, are just as undeserving of Your salvation and forgiveness. It is only through Your grace (Biblical definition – Something we do not deserve but receive anyway) and our faith that we receive the gift of salvation and forgiveness. Our heart's desire should be like Yours, wishing that none would perish but all would come to the saving knowledge of Jesus Christ.

Father, we know rebellion is the spirit of divination as You tell us in 1 Samuel 15:23. Proverbs 16:18 also tells us, *"Pride goes before destruction, and haughty spirit before stumbling."* Please Lord, keep our pride in check! Instead, let us be humble as it teaches in 1 Peter 5:6, *"Humble yourselves, therefore, under the mighty hand of God, that He may exalt you at the proper time."*

Isaiah 65:1 instructs, *"I [The Lord] permitted myself to be sought by those who did not ask for me; I permitted myself to be found by those who did not seek Me. I said, 'Here am I, here am I, to a nation which did not call on My name.'"* Father, Your heart is to seek those who are lost, people who do not believe in You, or understand You, or know who You are. Father, let us be like You and not like Jonah. Let us continue to pray for those who are lost and in desperate need of You, even though they do not know or understand what they are missing.

There is no greater joy than witnessing a Saul turned into a Paul, or Zacchaeus from tax collector to disciple, or Rahab from prostitute to an ancestor in the genealogy of Jesus. Thank you, Father, that You have given us many examples of what You expect of us. We, too, want to be spoken about like the great men and women in Hebrews 11 who gained Your approval by their faith. Let us be men and women of God who move mountains for the cause of Christ.

In the mighty name of Jesus.

REFLECTION

Review Jonah, chapters 3 and 4.

1. What was Jonah's attitude when the Lord told him to go to Nineveh the second time? (4:2-3)

   _____
   _____

2. How did the people respond to Jonah's message? (Jonah 3:5)

   _____
   _____

3. What happened because of the people doing as the Lord instructed? (Jonah 3:10)

   _____
   _____

4. What did Jonah care about more than the people? (Jonah 4:6-10)

   _____
   _____

5. What is more important to you than what God has called you to do? (money, athletics, your special talent, appearance, status, etc.)

   _____
   _____
   _____

PRAYER

Write your prayer against rebellion:

MY STORY
Power of Praying Parents

Thirteen years ago, my husband and I moved to Texas at the request of the owner of his company. The company did all they could to make the move as seamless as possible, including hiring a relocation company. Through them, we were also assigned a realtor to help us locate a new place to live. We spent a full day with our realtor and, although he was a nice person, he was not a good fit for us. On our next visit to Texas, I requested a different realtor who would better understand our style of living. The next morning, I met my lifelong friend, Julie.

Julie is a soft-spoken, petite blonde who is kind and friendly. She is also a sharp businesswoman who works hard to ensure her clients get the best in home purchases. During our first day, Julie

and I realized we had much in common. We both had adult children who sometimes did not exactly do as we would hope in situations. We both had grandsons we were crazy about, but neither of our daughters had been married when the children were born. Our daughters and their sons both lived with us following the births and for some time afterwards. Julie's daughter, Rachel, and grandson were still living with her and her husband, Keith.

Little by little, as we became better acquainted and more comfortable with each other, we learned more of each other's stories. Julie and Keith are a faithful Christian couple who raised their children to know and love the Lord. Somewhere along the way, their daughter decided to walk away from God and into the world of darkness and drugs.

Julie and Keith were in anguish over the fate of their daughter. They loved her so much, but had been hurt many times by her recklessness in her life and also in her son's life. They begged and pleaded, sponsored her in rehab programs, took care of her child, they threatened…but mostly they prayed.

They called in their prayer warrior friends and enlisted family members to pray. They begged and pleaded with God to save their daughter. They were getting to the end of their rope when they saw a glimpse of light.

This is how Julie and Keith explain in their own words God's faithfulness:

> "It's interesting how a continuous stream of stressful events might change your life. There are days of prayerful strength and others of just feeling dazed in the painful realization of what had happened to our beautiful daughter. Through all these days, we never gave up the belief we would see our daughter whole again and worked hard to not let her feel condemned, but yet let her know her path was not acceptable. Keith always stood on Acts 16:31, *'Believe on the Lord Jesus Christ, and you will be saved, you and your household.' AND YOUR HOUSEHOLD!* What a powerful reminder of God's faithfulness. During the days of deep darkness in throes of typical addiction behavior with a loved one, Julie tried various support groups. In her case, they were filled with stories of despair and failed attempts for loved ones to find long-term healing from their addictions. A decision was made to not look to man but to just pray and seek God."

> "Rachel was turned into CPS regarding the care of her son and, thankfully, custody of their grandson was given to Keith and Julie just days before a miracle happened in Rachel's life. Rachel's rebellion flared a couple nights later, but Keith was able to make her stay home knowing her intentions were to seek out a night of partying."

"Rachel actually was thinking it was time to flee; she was tired of living in the drug world but just didn't know how to turn away from years of this life. She turned to prayer that night, partly in anger and partly just out of complete despair. Praying even through the next day, 'God if You are real, do a work in my life.' We were so pleased that she agreed to go to church that afternoon for an evening service. The sermon was about secrets and the pastor had everyone hold hands and pray. Praise God something broke loose and God completely healed Rachel of her years of addiction! Were the weeks to come an easy path? NO! There was much healing and work in her life and ours as well. But those days were filled with God's precious encouragement!"

God has given Julie and Keith back their daughter. I have been blessed to spend a bit of time with Rachel, and she is the most evangelistic person I know. She is on fire for the Lord! There is no one with whom Rachel won't talk to or share the gospel. The waiter in the restaurant, the guy cleaning up at school, the lady at the cash register…all are fair game for Rachel's preaching. I can't wait to get to heaven and find out how many people are there because of the faithful parents who prayed for their child.

Julie and Keith prayed for their daughter to quit drugs, become a healthy adult, and take over the duties of raising her child. They were just praying for their desires and had no idea what God had in mind for their amazing daughter.

Maureen H Maldonado

ATTITUDINAL PRAYERS

Some passages in Scripture imply prayer, but the word prayer is not used. For example, John 17:1, *"These things Jesus spoke; and lifting His eyes to heaven, He said, . . ."* This is a clear indication Jesus was praying to the Father. Another example is Psalm 51:1-2, *"Be gracious to me, God, according to Thy lovingkindness according to the greatness of Thy compassion, blot out my transgressions. ² Wash me thoroughly from my iniquity and cleanse me from my sin."* David wrote this Psalm after He sinned with Bathsheba. David asking the Lord to cleanse him from sin is a prayer of repentance. These prayers are Attitudinal Prayers. The remainder of our prayers in the Old Testament will be Attitudinal Prayers; they are within the following texts:

- 1 Kings 3:5-10 – *"In Gibeon the Lord appeared to Solomon in a dream at night; and God said, "Ask what you wish Me to give you. And Solomon said,"*

- 1 Kings 8:22-24 – *"Then Solomon stood before the altar of the Lord in the presence of all the assembly of Israel, and he spread out his hands toward heaven. And he said,"*

- Psalm 25:16-22 – *"Turn to me and be gracious to me, For I am lonely and afflicted."*

- Psalm 51 - *"Be gracious to me, O God, according to Thy lovingkindness; according to the greatness of Thy compassion, blot out my transgressions."*

- Psalm 103:1-13 – *"Bless the Lord, O my soul, and all that is within me, bless His holy name. Bless the Lord my soul, and do not forget any of His benefits;"*

- Psalm 118:1-4; 15-24 – *"O Lord, do save us, we beseech Thee; O Lord, we beseech Thee, do send prosperity!"*

DAY 10
PRAYER FOR WISDOM

"⁵ In Gibeon the LORD appeared to Solomon in a dream at night; and God said, "Ask what you wish Me to give you."⁶ Then Solomon said, "Thou hast shown great lovingkindness to Thy servant David my father, according as he walked before Thee in truth and righteousness and uprightness of heart toward Thee; and Thou have reserved for him this great lovingkindness, that Thou hast given him a son to sit on his throne, as it is this day. ⁷ And now, O LORD my God, Thou have made Thy servant king in place of my father David, yet I am but a little child; I do not know how to go out or come in. ⁸ And Thy servant is in the midst of Thy people whom Thou hast chosen, a great people who cannot be numbered or counted for multitude. ⁹ So give Thy servant an understanding heart to judge Thy people, to discern between good and evil. For who is able to judge this great people of Thine? ¹⁰And it was pleasing in the sight of the Lord that Solomon had asked this thing."

1 Kings 3:5-10

CONTEXT

King Solomon was known for his wisdom, ability to lead, and his love for the Lord. He also had 700 wives. In our opinion, Solomon is one of the most confusing people in the Bible. Scripture tells us, even though he loved the Lord, he sacrificed and burned incense in the high places (worshipping other gods). Early in his reign, he had a conversation with God in a dream. The Lord told Solomon, *"Ask what you wish Me to give you."* (1 Kings 3:5). Regardless of the size of our leadership role, God's wisdom is vital in our daily lives.

PRAYER

Father, let us have a heart like Solomon that wishes to discern between good and evil. You teach in James 1:5, *"But if any of you lacks wisdom, let him ask of God, who gives to all men generously and without reproach, and it will be given to him."* We are asking for a generous portion of Your wisdom. We do not want the wisdom of the world; we want Your wisdom! You tell us in 1 Corinthians 1:25, *"Because the foolishness of God is wiser than men, and the weakness of God is stronger than men."* Let our lives be a reflection to the lost so they may see our heart's desire to follow You.

Father, we need wisdom in every area of our lives. We need wisdom in our families, friendships, workplaces, schools, and in everything we do. Please give us wisdom when voting for local, state, and national leaders.

Please give Your wisdom to all people in leadership. We especially pray today for wisdom for our politicians (1 Timothy 2:1-2), *"First of all, then, I urge that entreaties and prayers, petitions, and thanksgivings, be made on behalf of all men, for kings and all who are in authority, in order that we may lead a tranquil and quiet life in all godliness and dignity."*

Let us remember any wisdom we have is from you, Lord. Let us always give You glory and honor for blessing us. It is not of our ability, but only because You love us and have given us the gift of wisdom that we are successful. Let us always be like Daniel in Daniel 2:23 *"To Thee, O God of my fathers, I give thanks and praise, For Thou has given me wisdom and power."*

In the mighty name of Jesus.

REFLECTION

Review 1 Kings 3:6-9

1. How did Solomon describe the Lord? (v. 6)

   _____
   _____
   _____

2. To whom did Solomon give credit for making him king? (v. 7)

   _____
   _____
   _____

3. How does Solomon describe himself? (v.7)

   _____
   _____
   _____

4. What was Solomon's request of the Lord? (v. 9)

   _____
   _____
   _____

5. What would be your request of the Lord?

   _____
   _____
   _____

PRAYER

Write your prayer for wisdom:

DAY 11
PRAYER OF DEDICATION

"*²²Then Solomon stood before the altar of the Lord in the presence of all the assembly of Israel, and spread out his hands toward heaven. ²³And he said, "O Lord, the God of Israel, there is no God like You in heaven above or on earth beneath, keeping covenant and showing lovingkindness to Thy servants who walk before Thee with all their heart, ²⁴ who have kept with Thy servant, my father David, that which Thou promised him; indeed, Thou hast spoken with Thy mouth and hast fulfilled it with Thy hand as it is this day."*

1 Kings 8:22-24

CONTEXT

King David wanted to build a temple for the Lord, but the Lord specifically designated David's son, Solomon, to build the temple. The time had finally arrived, and the new temple was ready to open. Solomon wanted the event to be an amazing ceremony. For convenience so all could attend, it was scheduled when the faithful would be in the city to sell their crops. The Ark of the Covenant was the most important item to go into the temple, and it was carried in with all the pomp  and circumstance warranted. The temple had taken seven years to build. Here is the prayer of Solomon as he stood before the altar of the Lord and prayed to consecrate the temple.

PRAYER

Father, God, thank You that You are a covenant God, and that You are faithful when we are faithless (2 Timothy 2:13). Solomon built Your temple with brick and mortar, but You build Your temple in our hearts and lives. Our bodies are temples of the Holy Spirit if we belong to You. Therefore let us care for our bodies as living testimonies to others of Your greatness. We are Your servants: let us praise You evermore.

Ephesians 2:10 teaches, *"For we are His workmanship, created in Christ Jesus for good works, which God prepared beforehand, that we should walk in them."* Let us be diligent to go about our days fulfilling the calling You have placed upon our lives. You have set us apart from the world, but our roles are to be an example to the world.

We give You praise, glory, and honor in all we do. Let our lives be a shining example of Your presence in our lives. We desire to draw others to Your redemptive power and salvation, fulfilling

the commandment to go and make disciples (Matthew 28:19-20). We will teach them all You command. You have the authority, and You will be with us until the end of the age. We are dedicating ourselves to You and teaching others to dedicate themselves to You also.

Father, *"Let us do all things without grumbling or disputing, that you may prove to be blameless and innocent children of God, above reproach in the midst of a crooked and perverse generation, among whom you appear as lights to the world"* (Philippians 2:14-16). Let us hold fast to Your Word and let us not toil in vain.

We give you all the honor and glory in the mighty name of Jesus.

REFLECTION

Review 1 Kings 8:10-61

1. Why did Solomon build the temple instead of King David? (vv. 15-21)

   _____

   _____

   _____

2. How did Solomon describe the Lord? (v. 23)

   - _____

   - _____

   - _____

   - _____

3. Have you ever wanted to do something for God, yet it wasn't your assignment? Explain. What was the result?

   _____

   _____

   _____

   _____

   _____

   _____

   _____

   _____

PRAYER

Write your prayer of dedication:

DAY 12
PRAYER OF PROTECTION

"16 Turn to me and be gracious to me, for I am lonely and afflicted. 17 The troubles of my heart are enlarged; bring me out of my distresses. 18 Look upon my affliction and my trouble, and forgive all my sins. 19 Look upon my enemies, for they are many, and they hate me with violent hatred. 20 Guard my soul and deliver me; Do not let me be ashamed, for I take refuge in Thee. 21 Let integrity and uprightness preserve me, For I wait for Thee. 22 Redeem Israel, O God, Out of all his troubles."

Psalm 25:16-22

CONTEXT

We do not have much information on the Psalm of protection David wrote. But we do know David's history, and we know David needed protection! Saul tried to kill him multiple times. His son, Absolom, tried to kill him and overtake the kingdom. There was a time David found himself living in caves and was at war with several outlying countries. This Psalm could have been written during any of these periods, but it is clear David's trust was in the Lord. David was confident the Lord would never abandon him.

PRAYER

Father, God, I ask You to be gracious to me. I pray for Your protection. I need protection from (*insert your need*). When I am lonely and afraid, remind me to run to You because You are my ever-present help in time of need (Psalm 6:1). You tell us in Matthew 11:28, *"Come to Me (Jesus) all who are weary and heavy-laden, and I will give you rest. Take My yoke upon you and learn from Me, for I am gentle and humble in heart, and YOU WILL FIND REST FOR YOUR SOULS."*

The trials of life weigh me down and I need to find my rest in You. Father, help me come to You instead of looking elsewhere for solutions. Only then will I know true peace and release from these burdens. We thank You that You are my High Priest who sympathizes with my weakness. You have been tempted in all things as I am, yet without sin. Because of this, I can draw near to You with confidence to Your throne of grace and will receive mercy and grace to help in my time of need (Hebrews 4:15-16).

Lord, You tell us in Psalm 20:7, *"Some boast in chariots, and some in horses; but we will boast (trust) in the name of the Lord, our God."* I can find my comfort in You because You are my protector, my shield. You are my strength, and I am honored to take refuge in You. In you I will never be ashamed.

You are the God Most High. When I dwell in Your courts, no evil will penetrate me. You send Your angels to surround and protect me, and just like Daniel, You have the power to rescue me from the mouths of lions (Daniel 6:27). Because my trust is in You, I can sleep soundly under great affliction. Just like David in Psalm 25:20, when he says, *"Guard my soul and deliver me; do not let me be ashamed, for I take refuge in Thee,"* we also give You all honor and praise and wait for You, Our redeemer.

In the mighty name of Jesus.

Marta E Greenman *Maureen H Maldonado*

REFLECTION

Review Psalm 25

1. How was David feeling? (v. 16)

   _____

   _____

   _____

2. David asked the Lord to "look at" (v. 18):

My _____, my _____; (v. 19) Look at my _____ for they are many. They _____ me with a _____ _____.

3. David asked the Lord to do three things (v. 20)

   - _____
   - _____
   - _____

4. Who is your "go to" when you are lonely and afflicted? Give an example.

   _____

   _____

   _____

   _____

   _____

   _____

   _____

PRAYER

Write your prayer of protection:

MY STORY
Praying for a Miracle

As an American living in Romania, I learned something new every day! When we first moved into our apartment there were many lessons that helped me understand life in this former Communist country. One of the first enlightening moments was when it came to the water bill. The thought never occurred to me that we wouldn't have a separate water bill for each apartment.

Yet, all the apartments were the old Communist block style which meant shared water bills. At the end of each month the water company would read the meter and divide the total cost of the water bill by the number of apartments in the building.

Having my water consumption become a major source of contention between our neighbors was frightening. One night we heard voices yelling at one another outside. We looked out our window and saw all of our neighbors in our apartment yelling at a man standing on a bench. We sent someone down to find out what the commotion was and discovered that meeting was about us. The Americans!

The argument was about the water bill. Everyone's bill had skyrocketed. When we moved in, we installed a hot water tank in both the kitchen and the bathroom. We also had a daily feeding program for about 20 to 25 street children. After their lunch and a small Bible story, we provided clean cloths and a shower. The boys and girls alternated every other day, allowing the children to have two to three showers a week. This bill didn't include the water it took to wash all the clothes!

This much water consumption would raise anyone's water bill significantly. Our neighbors were ready to start a riot. Some of the elderly women in the block were living off the equivalent of $25 or $30 dollars a month. Their normal monthly water bill was less than 50 cents. Wanting to make a wrong right, I walked downstairs and advised the neighbors and the water man that tomorrow morning I would go down and pay the entire apartment block's water bill.

This event began a relationship with several neighbors. One woman was named Stefie. She was one of the older women living on a small government pension. Not long after the "water bill" event, I was looking out my window one morning and saw Stefie, sitting on the bench below. She opened up her coin purse, then closed it. Then she looked up at the sky, as if praying. When she finished, she opened her coin purse once again and her face became sad. She walked across the street and bought two loaves of bread. The cost would have been around ten cents in American dollars. The loaves are not American sized, and on average Romanians would eat approximately one half a loaf per meal.

This event made me realize Stefie had prayed for money to show up in her coin purse and it had not. Therefore she bought two loaves of bread which would be all she had to eat that day. What Stefie didn't realize was that God was answering her prayer, just not in the way she thought.

That night, just before we sat down for dinner, I made an extra plate of food and took it to Stefie. I explained to her that we had too much food and no room in the refrigerator. This comment would not have been out of the ordinary because most Romanians did not have American-sized refrigerators. A dorm-room size refrigerator would be a normal size at that time. Stefie looked so grateful, and somehow from that night on, we always seemed to have too much food to fit in the refrigerator.

God had allowed me to see Stefie's prayer and lovingly answer it without making her feel like a burden. Could God have placed extra money in Stefie's coin purse? Absolutely! Yet, God's ways are not our ways. His plan and purpose was to bring two women together, showing God's love and tender care for His creation.

Are you looking expectantly to the Lord for His answer to your prayers? Are you watching to see if the Lord wants YOU to be the instrument in answering someone's prayer? People are praying miracle prayers every day. God may want to use you to answer their need. I can promise you firsthand, you will be the one that is blessed.

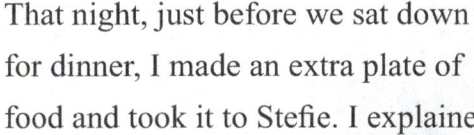

DAY 13
PRAYER OF REPENTANCE AND RESTORATION

"*¹Be gracious to me, O God, according to Thy lovingkindness; according to the greatness of Thy compassion blot out my transgressions. ² Wash me thoroughly from my iniquity, and cleanse me from my sin. ³ For I know my transgressions, and my sin is ever before me. ⁴ Against Thee, Thee only, I have sinned, and done what is evil in Thy sight, So that Thou art justified when Thou dost speak, And blameless when Thou dost judge. ⁵ Behold, I was brought forth in iniquity, and in sin my mother conceived me. ⁶ Behold, Thou dost desire truth in the innermost being, and in the hidden part Thou wilt make me know wisdom. ⁷ Purify me with hyssop, and I shall be clean; Wash me, and I shall be whiter than snow. 8 Make me to hear joy and gladness, Let the bones which Thou hast broken rejoice. ⁹ Hide Thy face from my sins, and blot out all my iniquities.*

¹⁰ Create in me a clean heart, O God, and renew a steadfast spirit within me. ¹¹ Do not cast me away from Thy presence, and do not take Thy Holy Spirit from me. ¹² Restore to me the joy of Thy salvation, and sustain me with a willing spirit. ¹³ Then I will teach transgressors Thy ways, and sinners will be converted to Thee. ¹⁴ Deliver me from bloodguiltiness, O God, Thou God of my salvation; Then my tongue will joyfully sing of Thy righteousness. ¹⁵ O Lord, open my lips, that my mouth may declare Thy praise. ¹⁶ For Thou dost not delight in sacrifice, otherwise I would give it; Thou art not pleased with burnt offering. ¹⁷ The sacrifices of God are a broken spirit; A broken and a contrite heart, O God, Thou wilt not despise. ¹⁸ By Thy favor do good to Zion; Build the walls of Jerusalem. ¹⁹ Then Thou wilt delight in righteous sacrifices, in burnt offering and whole burnt offering; Then young bulls will be offered on Thine altar."

Psalm 51

CONTEXT

This is the prayer David prayed after he had committed adultery with Bathsheba (the wife of Uriah the Hittite) and after he caused Uriah to be killed in battle to conceal that sin (2 Samuel 11:1-27).

PRAYER

Father, I thank You that You are a God who hears us, a God who loves us and does not want us to stay in our sinful natures. You want us to repent and return to You and restore the sweetness of restoration You bring. As Jabez prayed, please keep me from harm and the evil one: we pray this for our lives (1 Chronicles 4:10). And as Jesus taught us in Matthew 6:14, we are to forgive others so our heavenly Father will forgive us. Let us be quick to forgive and quick to ask for forgiveness.

Scripture teaches us through Adam that all men have sinned, and as believers we are not immune. As David said, give me a willing spirit to walk in Your ways (Psalm 51:12). However, when I stumble and fall, let me run to You and confess my sin before You, my great High Priest, and know that You will cleanse me and lead me on a righteous path.

Father, let me run to the foot of the cross, where I know I will be washed with the blood of Jesus. Let us be like the great saints in Revelation 7:14 and be worthy of the white robes given to us that have been washed white in the blood of the Lamb.

Thank You, Father, for a clean heart and a renewed spirit. Thank You that You have cast my sins as far as the east is from the west (Psalm 103:12). Thank You that I can have joy with a renewed spirit. Let me be an example of who You are and what You have done in my life. Lord, help

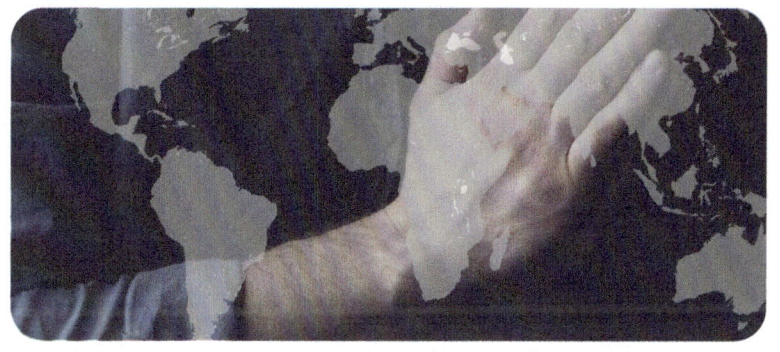

me teach transgressors Your ways and lead sinners to the foot of the cross so they, too, can find Your compassion, grace, and mercy. Let us be humble in spirit, for You give grace to the humble, but the proud You bring low (James 4:6; 1 Peter 5:5). Let us daily draw near to You, who can keep our feet from stumbling, and may we always give You praise, honor, and glory in Your Son's holy name.

In the mighty name of Jesus.

Marta E Greenman *Maureen H Maldonado*

REFLECTION

Review Psalm 25

1. Whom did David say he has sinned against? (v. 4)

   _____

2. Did David fully admit his sin, or did he try to cover it up?

   _____

   List what David said about his sin:

   (v. 1) _____ out my transgressions.
   (v. 2) Wash me thoroughly from my _____. _____ me from my sin.
   (v. 3) I know my _____, and my _____ is ever before me.
   (v. 4) Against thee I have _____ and done what is _____ in thy sight.

3. Whom did David say is able to judge and why (v. 4)?

   _____

4. For what did David ask in verses 10-12?
   _____ in me a clean heart, _____ a steadfast spirit,
   Do not _____ _____ me away from my presence.
   Do not _____ - _____ Thy holy spirit from me.
   _____ to me the ___ of Thy salvation.
   _____ me with a _____ spirit. (v. 12)
   Result: Then I will _____ transgressors Your ways. (v. 13)
   And sinners will be _____ to You. (v. 13)

5. What kind of sacrifice does the Lord expect? (v. 17)

   - _____

   - _____

PRAYER

Write your prayer of repentance and restoration:

DAY 14
PRAYER OF PRAISE AND REMEMBRANCE

"¹Bless the Lord, O my soul, and all that is within me, bless His holy name. ² Bless the Lord, my soul, and forget none of His benefits; ³ Who pardons all your iniquities, Who heals all your diseases; ⁴ Who redeems your life from the pit, Who crowns you with lovingkindness and compassion;

⁵ Who satisfies your years with good things, so that your youth is renewed like the eagle. ⁶ The Lord performs righteous deeds and judgments for all who are oppressed. ⁷ He made known His ways to Moses, His acts to the sons of Israel. ⁸ The Lord is compassionate and gracious, Slow to anger and abounding in lovingkindness. ⁹ He will not always strive with us, nor will He keep His anger forever. ¹⁰ He has not dealt with us according to our sins, nor rewarded us according to our iniquities. ¹¹ For as high as the heavens are above the earth, so great is His lovingkindness toward those who fear Him. ¹² As far as the east is from the west, so far has He removed our transgressions from us. ¹³ Just as a father has compassion on his children, so the Lord has compassion on those who fear Him. ¹⁴ For He Himself knows our frame; He is mindful that we are but dust."

Psalm 103:1-14

CONTEXT

Not much is known about Psalm 103, except in this Psalm, David praised God for everything He had done for David. This prayer is a clear indication of David's heart and a great reminder for all of us.

PRAYER

Father God, You are the God who is holy, and You have called us to be holy as You are holy. We are blessed that You look after every need in our daily lives. Psalm 103 tells us not to forget any of Your benefits. I praise You because You are the only God who can forgive our sins, the only One who can heal our diseases, and the only One who can transform us. I thank You that You redeemed my life from the pit when I was making bad decisions and living life recklessly apart from You.

I thank You for Your lovingkindness and compassion and know You are the only One who can satisfy my days. I thank You that You will take the follies of my youth and redeem them so I will be able to soar like the eagle.

Lord, only You can perform righteous deeds. Your judgments are true. Father, just as You made known Your ways to Moses, I ask You to make Your ways known to me. I thank You that You are compassionate and gracious. Without You being slow to anger, Your judgment would have been upon my life. Instead, I receive new mercies every morning.

Father, we know Your patience will not last forever, therefore while we have the opportunity, let us grab ahold of Your grace and mercy and repent of our wicked ways. We will not receive rewards for our iniquities, but through Christ's death on the cross and our faith in His salvation, our sins will not be counted against us. Let us be children who fear You in reverence and awe. I thank You that when we repent, You remove our transgressions as far as the east is from the west. You are a good Father who has compassion on Your children and compassion upon those who fear You. We thank You that You have made Yourself known to us so that we may praise You all the day long.

We pray this in the mighty name of Jesus.

Marta E Greenman   *Maureen H Maldonado*

REFLECTION

Review Psalm 103:1-14

1. List the benefits of the Lord. (vv. 1-5) He...

   - _____
   - _____
   - _____
   - _____
   - _____

2. List the adjectives describing the Lord. (vv. 4-13)

   _____ and _____,

   (v. 8) _____ and _____,

   (v. 8) slow to _____ and abounding in _____.

   (v. 11) _____ toward those who fear Him.

   (v. 13) _____ on those who fear Him.

3. What attribute is the Lord displaying most in your life right now? Give details.

PRAYER

Write your prayer of praise and remembrance:

DAY 15
PRAYER OF THANKSGIVING

"Give thanks to the Lord, for He is good; For His lovingkindness is everlasting. 2 Oh let Israel say, 'His lovingkindness is everlasting.' 3 Oh let the house of Aaron say, 'His lovingkindness is everlasting.' 4 Oh let those who fear the Lord say, 'His lovingkindness is everlasting.'"

"And He has become my salvation. ¹⁵ The sound of joyful shouting and salvation is in the tents of the righteous; The right hand of the LORD does valiantly. ¹⁶ The right hand of the LORD is exalted; The right hand of the LORD performs valiantly. ¹⁷ I will not die, but live, and tell of the works of the LORD. ¹⁸ The LORD has disciplined me severely, but He has not turned me over to death. ¹⁹ Open to me the gates of righteousness; I shall enter through them, I shall give thanks to the LORD. ²⁰ This is the gate of the LORD; The righteous will enter through it. ²¹ I shall give thanks to Thee, for Thou hast answered me, and Thou hast become my salvation. ²² The stone which the builders rejected has become the chief cornerstone. ²³ This is the LORD'S doing; It is marvelous in our eyes. ²⁴ This is the day which the LORD has made; Let's rejoice and be glad in it."

Psalm 118:1-4; 14b-24

CONTEXT

Most Biblical scholars believe Psalm 118 was written by King David. This psalm was written during a period of rejoicing; Israel's enemies had been defeated and David had begun to reign as King. The Psalmist begins by telling all to, *"Give thanks to the Lord, for He is good; For His lovingkindness is everlasting"* (Psalm 118:1). The praises of the Lord continued throughout the times of difficulty when it became *"Better to take refuge in the Lord than to trust in man"* (Psalm 118:8). By calling on the name of the Lord, the nations that came against Israel were cut off and God was praised and thanked for the day that was good. Psalm 118 is often sung during Passover to celebrate the Israelites being led out of captivity and protected daily by God.

PRAYER

We give You thanks for the beautiful sunrises and beautiful sunsets, the majestic mountains, and spectacular oceans. We stand in awe that You lavish Your love upon us daily. We thank You that Your lovingkindness is everlasting, and we do not fear because we are Yours.

Father, we thank You that You have given us a voice to proclaim Your works. Your Word tells us we overcome by the blood of the Lamb and the word of our testimony (Revelation 12:11). We thank You that even Your discipline is for our own good. *"For they [fathers] disciplined us for a short time as seemed best to them, but He disciplines us for our good, that we may share His holiness"* (Hebrews 12:10). Father, we ask that You allow righteousness to rule in our lives.

We thank You for every answer to every prayer. We thank You for family. We thank You for finances that put a roof over our heads and pay for our basic needs. We thank You for healthy minds and bodies so we may enjoy all Your blessings and do Your work here on earth.

We thank You for the Bible written in a language we can read and understand. We thank You that you have given us a mind to meditate upon Your Word. Thank You for Your peace, even in the midst of turbulent times.

Father, let us rejoice daily that You have given us another day with breath in our bodies, another day to proclaim Your goodness, another day to labor for You and tell of Your grace and mercy. We thank You that even in difficult days, we can cry out to You and You will hear us and comfort us as only You can. Father, let us not waste the days, but let every moment be ordained by You that we may walk forward and bring You glory.

In the mighty name of Jesus.

Marta E Greenman   *Maureen H Maldonado*

REFLECTION

Review Psalm 118

1. How many days are made by the Lord? How many of them are good days?

   _____
   _____
   _____
   _____
   _____

2. Why was David giving thanks to the Lord?

   _____
   _____
   _____
   _____
   _____

3. Note a time when you had a really good day and write why it was good.

   _____
   _____
   _____
   _____
   _____
   _____

PRAYER

Write your prayer of Thanksgiving:

PrayerFULL

SECTION TWO
NEW TESTAMENT

αἴτημα
aitema

Philippians 4:6 is our Scripture reference for the Greek word aitema.

"Be anxious for nothing, but in everything by prayer and supplication with thanksgiving let your requests (aitema) be made known to God." We are using the word "requests" for our example. It means, "that which is being asked for - 'request, demand, what was being asked for.'[5]"

---

[1] Johannes P. Louw and Eugene Albert Nida, *Greek-English Lexicon of the New Testament: Based on Semantic Domains* (New York: United Bible Societies, 1996), 406.

OUR STORY
Becoming PrayerFULL
Maureen, Part 1

I believed that the reason God has allowed Marta and me to write this book is to help you, the reader, learn how to pray using Scripture. Isn't it just like God to teach me while going through the process! I am here to tell you that this book has so impacted me! Marta and I have written this manuscript together. Each page, and every word, except our personal stories, have been written together. When we question wording, there is always a word or words that just grab me! Actually, I think that has occurred in each day's devotional. God removes some scales from my eyes and my heart as I get more deeply into Scripture.

For example, the day we were writing the Prayer of the Afflicted, within fifteen minutes after we had finished writing, I had a call from someone I love who was in deep distress. There was nothing I could physically do to solve the problem, but I was able to listen, encourage, and share with her what we had just written about Hannah. Hannah took her heartache to the Lord and He freed her from her sadness. Then I prayed.

There was the day we wrote the Prayer of Jabez. I am very familiar with the prayer of Jabez as I have a tapestry on my wall which was a gift from my sister, Colleen, many years ago. I did not really understand, until the day we wrote the Prayer of Jabez, the extreme type of poverty Jabez was born into or the futility of his name which means "born in pain." We all struggle with something at some time in our lives. We just need to do as Jabez and take it to the Lord. We need to ask HIM to enlarge our territory and keep His hand over us.

There are over 130 verses in the Bible about knowledge and/or wisdom. We can never get enough of either. In 1 Kings 3:3-9, Solomon asked the Lord to give him wisdom. James 1:5 tells us, "*If any of you lacks wisdom, let him ask of God, who gives to all men generously and without reproach, and it (wisdom) will be given to him.*" Ecclesiastes 9:16 teaches wisdom is better than strength. As we were working on the Prayer for Wisdom, I felt a strong tug-of-war between myself and the enemy who tries to stop us at every turn when we get closer to the Lord. I found myself praying constantly for the wisdom to continue writing this book and the wisdom to make the best decisions about sending His message to you.

Moral of the story: … pray … always … constantly … about everything. I cannot describe to you the peace I feel when I spend time with the Lord. Oh! And by the way, our next book is PeaceFULL, be sure and watch for it. He is waiting for you to come to Him!

Maureen H. Maldonado

OUR STORY
Becoming PrayerFULL
Marta, Part 2

I have long felt God calling me to write devotionals and was thrilled when our first one, *FearLESS,* was published. I have wanted to write a book teaching others how to pray Scripture for many years. Why? Because I know the impact this simple, yet powerful tool has made in my life. I often say prayer is our first weapon of warfare. Prayer pole-vaults us into the spiritual realm instead of holding us to the earthly realm. When we learn to pray effective prayers, we will see life through spiritual eyes instead of earthly eyes. Prayer changes the entire dynamic on how to live, what we believe, and what can be accomplished through God's mighty hand. *"Jesus said to them, 'With people this is impossible, but with God all things are possible'"* (Matthew 19:26). Prayer helps us understand, and to see firsthand that with God, all things are possible!

Writing *PrayerFULL* with Maureen has allowed me to see the fruit of many prayers over many years. What is the secret to a successful prayer life? Knowing and praying Scripture. That sounds simple and it may be, but 1 John 5:14-15 says, *"This is the confidence which we have before Him, that, if we ask anything according to His will, He hears us. And if we know that He hears us in whatever we ask, we know that we have the requests which we have asked from Him."* If we want confidence in our prayer life, we need to ask according to His will. How do we know God's will? We know from Scripture, when we pray Scripture, we are praying the heart of God.

As someone who was raised in the church but didn't come to know the Lord until the age of 29, I knew I needed power behind my request. Almost 30 years ago, I said a 911 prayer, you know what I mean, a desperate prayer pleading with God to show me how to pray. His answer was simple, pray Scripture! I have prayed His word ever since. God is faithful. Do you want to move mountains? Pray Scripture. Nothing is impossible with God.

Marta E Greenman

DAY 16
PRAY ABOUT EVERYTHING

"⁴Rejoice in the Lord always; again I will say, rejoice! ⁵ Let your forbearing spirit be known to all men. The Lord is near. ⁶ Be anxious for nothing, but in everything by prayer and supplication with thanksgiving let your requests be made known to God. ⁷ And the peace of God, which surpasses all comprehension, shall guard your hearts and your minds in Christ Jesus. ⁸ Finally, brethren, whatever is true, whatever is honorable, whatever is right, whatever is pure, whatever is lovely, whatever is of good repute, if there is any excellence and if anything worthy of praise, let your mind dwell on these things. ⁹ The things you have learned and received and heard and seen in me, practice these things; and the God of peace shall be with you."

Philippians 4:4-9

CONTEXT

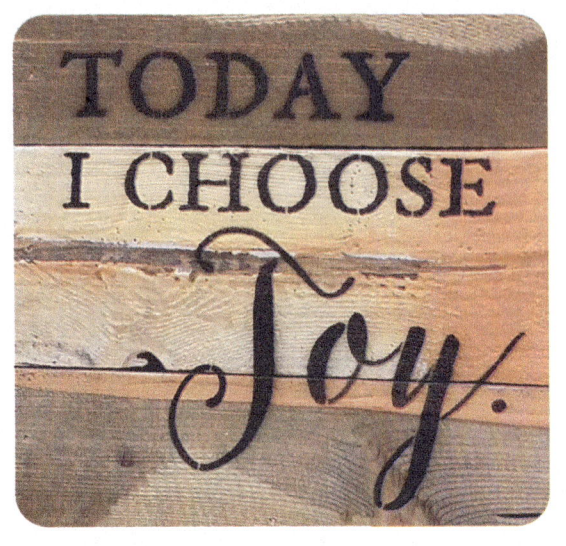

Biblical historians believe Paul wrote Philippians while in prison in Rome from 60-62 A.D. He wrote this letter to remind the faithful of things he knew to be true. The contradiction here is that this letter is often referred to as "joyful," but he was actually in prison, not a joyous situation. Key words in this epistle were "joy" used 7 times, and "rejoice" used 7 times. The audience was to rejoice in the Lord always, to be anxious (*merimnao*) about nothing, and to pray for everything.

PRAYER

Father God, I thank You that You are a God we can rejoice in! We can rejoice when others are in sorrow because we know You are in control. When we are Yours, we rejoice because we have life eternal. We can rejoice because You are always near. We can rejoice because You are the God of peace and comfort. Father, let us be good examples of You and what You have done in our lives. Even in our darkest days, please let me direct all glory and honor to You.

Father, let us guard our hearts and minds in Christ. Let us dwell on You and not on the things of the world which can so easily weigh us down. Just as the apostle Paul

was able to rejoice even while imprisoned, help us to rejoice even in the difficult times of our lives.

Father, You tell us to *"Be anxious for nothing but in everything by prayer and supplication with thanksgiving let your requests be known to God"* (Philippians 4:6.)

I thank You that I can bring everything from the smallest issue to the largest mountain to Your attention. What others may think as trivial or meaningless, I know You care as much for my petitions, regardless how large or small (Philippians 4:6).

Father, let my speech be honoring to You. Let me say only that which is true. Yet, if it is true but not honorable, let me keep silent. Let me live a pure and righteous life pleasing to You, a life which would lead others to speak highly of my reputation (Proverbs 22:1). I think of Daniel when he was serving the pagan kings in Babylon. Scripture tells us he had favor in the sight of those in authority even though his beliefs were contrary to those of the kings (Daniel 1:9, Daniel 6:26).

Father, let us practice the things we have learned in Your Word, so You, the God of peace, will be with us always. Father, I pray for (prayer request).

In the mighty name of Jesus.

REFLECTION

Review Philippians 4:4-9

1. Give an example of how you can rejoice in times of difficulty.

   _____
   _____
   _____
   _____

2. How does the God of peace help when anxiety threatens to steal your peace?

   _____
   _____
   _____
   _____

3. Scripture tells us to pray about everything. Is that easy or difficult for you and why?

   _____
   _____
   _____
   _____
   _____

PRAYER

Write your prayer about everything:

δέομαι
deomai

Acts 4:24-31 is our Scripture reference for the Greek word deomai.

This means "to ask for with urgency, with the implication of presumed need - to plead, to beg."

[6] *Johannes P. Louw and Eugene Albert Nida, Greek-English Lexicon of the New Testament: Based on Semantic Domains (New York: United Bible Societies, 1996), 407.*

DAY 17
PRAYER OF BOLDNESS

"²⁴And when they heard this, they lifted their voices to God with one accord and said, 'O Lord, it is Thou who didst made the heaven and the earth and the sea, and all that is in them, ²⁵ who by the Holy Spirit, through the mouth of our father David Thy servant, didst say,' Why did the Gentiles rage, And the peoples devise futile things?

The kings of the earth took their stand, and the rulers were gathered together against the Lord and against His Christ.' ²⁷ 'For truly in this city there were gathered together against Thy holy servant Jesus, whom Thou didst anoint, both Herod and Pontius Pilate, along with the Gentiles and the peoples of Israel, ²⁸ to do whatever Thy hand and Thy purpose predestined to occur. ²⁹And now, Lord, take note of their threats, and grant that Thy bondservants may speak Thy word with all confidence, ³⁰ while Thou dost extend Thy hand to heal, and signs and wonders take place through the name of Thy holy servant Jesus.' ³¹ And when they had prayed, the place where they had gathered together was shaken, and they were all filled with the Holy Spirit and began to speak the word of God with boldness."

Acts 4:24-31

CONTEXT

Following Jesus' ascension into heaven and when the Holy Spirit appeared at Pentecost, Peter and John healed a lame man. The crowds were full of amazement, and Peter and John glorified God and credited Him for the miracle. The Pharisees and Sadducees were highly disturbed that Peter and John were teaching the people and proclaiming in Jesus the resurrection of the dead. So they laid hands upon them (arrested them) and put them in jail. After being brought before the Council, Peter  and John were ordered not to speak about Jesus among the people, and they were beaten and released. Peter and John returned to their friends and reported all the events. When their friends heard everything that had happened, they began to pray and glorify the Lord.

PRAYER

Father, in these difficult days in which we are living, it is easier to shrink back than it is to stand boldly for You. John 10:10 tells us, *"The thief comes only to steal, and kill and destroy; I came that they may have life, and might have it abundantly."* There are only two forces at work in this world, light or darkness, good or evil. If we do not stand for light, darkness will prevail. Give us spiritual eyes to see everything clearly from world events to our personal day-to-day interactions as You see them. There is only one answer to every problem we are facing, and that answer is Jesus. We live in a world that desperately needs Your power, Your presence, and Your sovereignty. Let us give all glory to God in everything we do; let us do it for You and You alone.

Give us the strength to be like Peter, John, and their friends to make the decision to boldly proclaim Your truth no matter what the cost. When threats come our way, let us leave vengeance

to you. Romans 12:19 teaches, *"Never take your own revenge, beloved, but leave room for the wrath of God, for it is written, 'Vengeance is mine, I will repay,' says the Lord."*

You are the God who heals spiritually, emotionally, and physically. You chose us before the foundations of the earth to be Your agents of light. Let us be like Jesus as we go about our daily lives. Let us teach Your Word, proclaim the gospel of the kingdom of God, and heal in the name of Jesus spiritually, emotionally, and physically. Your Word tells is in Matthew 9:37, *"The harvest is plentiful but the workers are few."* Let it be said of us that we were bold workers for the cause of Christ.

In the mighty name of Jesus.

Marta E Greenman   *Maureen H Maldonado*

REFLECTION

Review Acts 4:24-31

1. What was the request of Peter and his friends according to verses 29 and 30?

   _____
   _____
   _____
   _____

2. What was the result of their prayer?

   _____
   _____
   _____
   _____

3. Who is in your friend group who will always bring you back to the Word of God?

   _____
   _____
   _____

4. Are you the friend who brings people back to the Word of God?

   _____
   _____
   _____
   _____

PRAYER

Write your prayer of boldness:

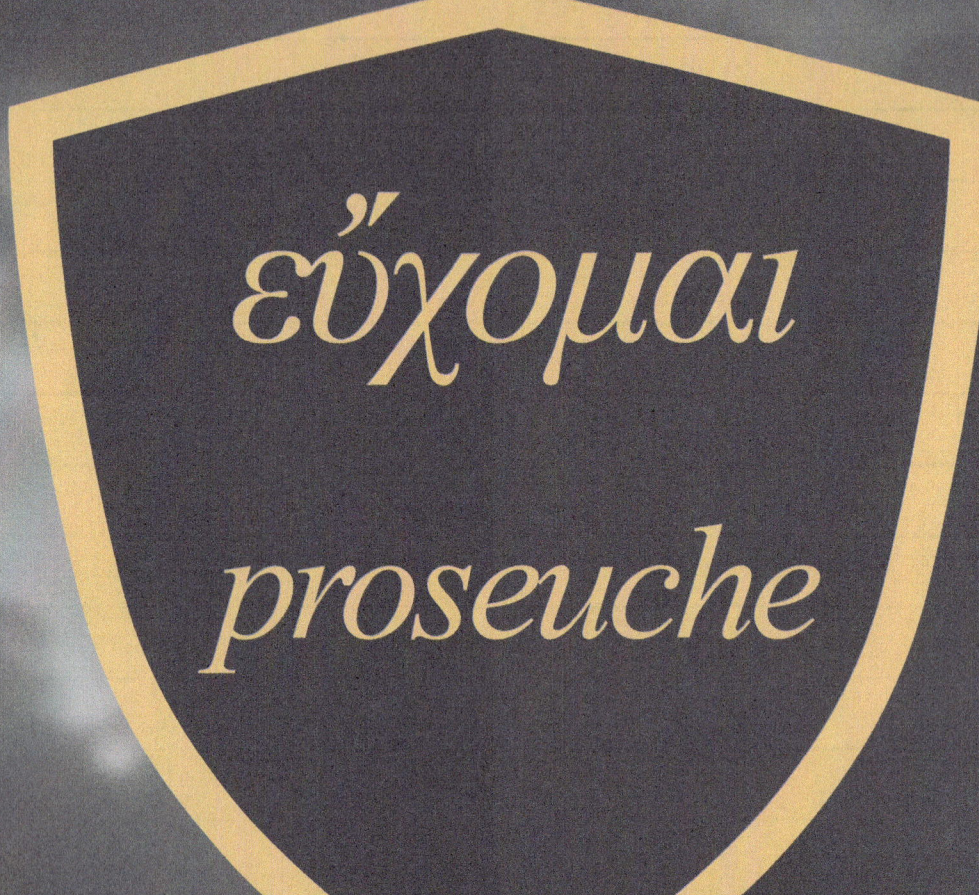

Acts 12:5 and 1 Timothy 2:1-3 are the Scripture references for the Greek word proseuche.

This simply means, "To speak to or to make requests of God—'to pray, to speak to God, to ask God for, prayer.⁷"

---

[7] Johannes P. Louw and Eugene Albert Nida, *Greek-English Lexicon of the New Testament: Based on Semantic Domains* (New York: United Bible Societies, 1996), 408.

DAY 18
PRAYER OF THE FAITHFUL

"⁵So Peter was kept in the prison, but prayer for him was being made fervently by the church to God."

"¹²And when he realized this, he went to the house of Mary, the mother of John, who was also called Mark, where many were gathered together and were praying."

Acts 12:5, 12

CONTEXT

In approximately 44 A.D., 11 years after Jesus' death, burial, and resurrection, the church was under severe persecution. Many Jews had already scattered throughout the region. The Gentiles had also received the Holy Spirit, and Herod Agrippa the first had put James, the brother of John, to death by the sword to please the Jews. Peter was arrested during the holy days of unleavened bread. After many days in prison, Peter found himself miraculously freed through the fervent prayers of the church.

PRAYER

Father, thank You that no matter what is happening around us or to us, we can know You are still in control. You are the King of Kings and Lord of Lords who sits on the throne. You remove kings and establish kings (Daniel 2:21).

Just like Peter's companions, let us always remember to be faithful in praying for others in the church who are being mistreated at the hands of others, like Peter's companions who were fervently in prayer for him. Today there are over 360 million Christians being persecuted for the cause of Christ. Many are held captive or beaten and threatened with death. Father, we pray on their behalf. Just as You sent Jesus, the Angel of the Lord, please send Your Angel of the Lord to them to miraculously loosen their chains and allow them to walk away free. Until they are freed, Lord, give them Your strength and perseverance to withstand everything the enemy casts on them. Let them be Your witness to other prisoners and to the jailers — leading them to knowledge of You as Paul and Silas did.

We pray for their persecutors, that they will come to know the Lord, Yeshua (עושי), as Lord and Savior. We pray they will repent and turn to You.

Father, let us be praying men and women of God. Let us expect miracles in Your name. Your Word tells us You are the same yesterday, today, and forever. Therefore, since You miraculously released Peter, You are able to do the same today.

Let us be diligent to go and tell of Your mighty signs and wonders so others will come to know You in Your saving power and saving grace. Father, we leave the persecutors in Your mighty hands. Your Word tells us, *"Vengeance is Mine, I will repay, but let us be faithful to not return evil for evil but evil for good"* (Romans 12:19b,21).

Let Your name always be given all the glory and let us move forward in faith until the whole world knows who You are!

In the mighty name of Jesus.

Marta E Greenman   *Maureen H Maldonado*

REFLECTION

Review Acts 12:24-31

1. While the church was fervently praying for Peter, what was he doing? (v. 6)

   _____

   _____

2. How many did Herod have guarding Peter? (v. 6)

   _____

   _____

3. Who came to Peter's rescue? (v. 7-8)

   _____

   _____

4. Peter was rescued from Herod and from all that the Jewish people were expecting. What do you think they were expecting? (v. 11)

   _____

   _____

5. What happened to Herod because he did not give God the glory? (v. 23)

   _____

   _____

6. What happened to the church and the Word of the Lord? (v. 24)

   _____

   _____

PRAYER

Write your prayer of the faithful:

DAY 19
PRAYER FOR THOSE IN AUTHORITY

"¹First of all, then, I urge that entreaties and prayers, petitions and thanksgivings, be made on behalf of all men, ² for kings and all who are in authority, in order that we may lead a tranquil and quiet life in all godliness and dignity. ³ This is good and acceptable in the sight of God our Savior, ⁴ who desires all men to be saved and to come to the knowledge of the truth. ⁵ For there is one God, and one mediator also between God and men, the man Christ Jesus, ⁶ who gave Himself as a ransom for all, the testimony born at the proper time. ⁷ And for this I was appointed a preacher and an apostle (I am telling the truth, I am not lying) as a teacher of the Gentiles in faith and truth. ⁸ Therefore I want the men in every place to pray, lifting up holy hands, without wrath and dissension."

1 Timothy 2:1-8

CONTEXT

It is believed Paul was living in Macedonia when he wrote his letters to Timothy, who was ministering in Ephesus. The letter was full of instructions about how Christians should live. Paul also charged them to pray for those in authority. Timothy was to use this information in his ministry to the church. Since these were Paul's instructions to Timothy, they are also God's instructions to us.

PRAYER

Father, I thank You that You establish kings and remove Kings (Daniel 2:21). You also give wisdom and knowledge to those in authority. I thank You for Paul's reminder to pray for those in authority, so we may lead a tranquil and quiet life (1Timothy 2:2). Father, I pray now specifically for President _____ (or leader of your country), that he or she has wisdom and discernment to run the government in a godly manner. If they do not know You, I pray they come to know You as Lord and Savior.

Your Word tells us when the righteous lead, the people rejoice (Proverbs 29:2). I pray for _____, the governor of my state. I pray for wisdom to flow down into all branches of government, national, state, and local. Father, I pray we all know there is one God, and we serve only Him. There is one mediator between God and man and His name is Jesus Christ (1 Timothy 2: 5). Let them come to understand that He gave Himself as a ransom

for us. Father, let us be diligent to preach the gospel in season and out of season. Let us pray continually for leaders with whom we agree and leaders with whom we do not agree.

Father, we pray also for people in non-elected authority positions. This list includes, but is certainly not limited to parents, corporation presidents, teachers, supervisors, anyone in a position to lead, have authority over, or be responsible for others. We pray for a generous helping of wisdom. Let them have love, joy, peace, patience, kindness, goodness, faithfulness, gentleness, and self-control (Galatians 5:22-23). Let them serve as You would serve, love as You would love, and judge by the plumbline of the Word of God. Most of us will be a leader in some capacity. Let us never forget the greatest leaders are those who are the greatest servants. Let us serve as Jesus served, looking to Him who is the author and perfecter of our faith (Hebrews 12:2).

In the mighty name of Jesus.

Marta E Greenman   *Maureen H Maldonado*

REFLECTION

Review 1 Timothy 2:1-8

1. Why do you think Paul said it was important to pray for those in authority? (v. 2).

   _____
   _____
   _____
   _____
   _____

2. What does verse 4 tell us about God's desire?

   _____
   _____
   _____
   _____
   _____

3. Who is our mediator, high priest, Savior? What benefit does He provide us?

   _____
   _____
   _____
   _____
   _____
   _____

PRAYER

Write your prayer for those in authority:

προσεύχομαι

proseuchomai

The Greek word Proseuchoma is used 87 times in the New Testament. We have chosen five Scriptures as our examples: Matthew 6:9-13, Matthew 26:39-42, Acts 9:11, Acts 16:24-26, and Colossians 1:9-12.

Proseuchomai simply means, "to speak to or to make requests of God—'to pray, to speak to God, to ask God for, prayer. In some languages there are a number of different terms used for prayer depending upon the nature of the content, for example, requests for material blessing, pleas for spiritual help, intercession for others, thanksgiving, and praise. There may also be important distinctions on the basis of urgency and need. The most generic expression for prayer may simply be 'to speak to God.' It is normally best to avoid an expression which means primarily 'to recite.'"[8]

Johannes P. Louw and Eugene Albert Nida, *Greek-English Lexicon of the New Testament: Based on Semantic Domains* (New York: United Bible Societies, 1996), 408.

MY STORY
Praying Grandmas

My pastor often talks about the power of praying grandmas. I am here to tell you that there is nothing more powerful I can do as a grandma than pray for my grandchildren. I can spoil them with material things and good food, and I can love them unconditionally, but my best gift to them is prayer.

I have an 18-year-old granddaughter, Eliza, whom I love very much. Eliza is one of those amazing human beings who gets exceptional grades in school, is kind to everyone, and is as beautiful inside as she is outside. As a young child, she would visit us for a week at a time which was always a highlight of our summers. She had a bedroom in our house, but often made her way into our bedroom and climbed into bed to sleep with us. To have three of us in the bed together was never comfortable for us but my husband and I did not mind.

As she has grown up, Eliza still likes to come visit us, and it is a weird feeling when she drives up to our house in her little car all by herself. Now she comes on the weekend and stays just one or two nights, depending on her schedule. Instead of cooking for her, I take her grocery shopping to buy vegetables or fruit, which she cooks in keeping with her specialized eating plan for her health and dancing. She was diagnosed with a kidney problem, and she will eventually need a transplant, so healthy eating is of upmost importance. We usually splurge with a trip for a frozen ICEE, which really means I get her in the car for 20 minutes uninterrupted.

Only a grandparent can know what I am talking about. There is just something so special about spending one-on-one time with the children of our children. Teenagers are often their own strange breed, so if they want to be with you AND want to talk with you, it is just a blessing.

Eliza is, however, a human teenager, and her mom is just doing her "mom" job when she checks to make sure schoolwork is complete, her room is clean, or house rules are followed. Every now and then, Eliza messes up – it's that human thing! Here it gets tricky, and prayer is the only answer. I NEVER take sides when there is an issue with mother and daughter, but I do see it from both viewpoints. I love them both so much that it hurts me when they are not in a good place. So, I do what is best, I pray.

I begin by thanking God for my children and grandchildren. I thank Him they are all well and leading good lives. I pray this scripture, *"Ah Lord God! Behold, Thou hast made the heavens and the earth by Thy great power and by Thine outstretched arm! Nothing is too difficult for Thee...'Behold, I am the Lord, The God of all Flesh. Is anything too hard for Me?"* (Jeremiah 32:17, 27 ESV). It always reminds me God is in control. He loves those children and grandchildren so much more than I ever could. He will take care of them; He will lead them to be productive citizens. He will get them through adolescence, and He has inscribed them in the palm of His hand as it says in Isaiah 49:16.

Never stop praying for those you love, especially your grandchildren! The big ones need you the most.

Maureen H Maldonado

DAY 20
THE LORD'S PRAYER

"⁷And when you are praying, do not use meaningless repetition as the Gentiles do, for they suppose that they will be heard for their many words. ⁸ Therefore do not be like them; for your Father knows what you need before you ask Him."

The Lord's Prayer

"⁹ Pray, then, in this way: 'Our Father, who is in heaven, Hallowed be Thy name. ¹⁰ Thy kingdom come. Thy will be done, on earth as it is in heaven. ¹¹ Give us this day our daily bread. ¹² And forgive us our debts, as we also have forgiven our debtors. ¹³ And do not lead us into temptation, but deliver us from evil. [For Thine is the kingdom, and the power, and the glory, forever. Amen]'"

Matthew 6:7-13

CONTEXT

This quotation is part of the famous Sermon on the Mount which was Jesus' first recorded sermon to the crowds. You can read the entire sermon from Matthew 5:1 to Matthew 7:29. Jesus covers crucial topics of murder, adultery, divorce, prayer, forgiveness, salvation, priorities, judgment, money, and many more. Matthew 7:29 tells us, *"He (Jesus) was teaching as one having authority, not as their scribes."* In other words, Jesus was not just the messenger.

PRAYER

Father, You are lifted high. You are the King of kings and Lord of lords. We praise and honor You. Your kingdom come, Father. Your will be done, on earth as it is in heaven. Therefore, let us ask Your will, let us find Your will and let us do Your will. Your will is our purpose when You set us apart for Yourself.

Your purpose in heaven should be our focus on earth. The prayer Jesus taught to His disciples says, *"Our Father, Who art in heaven."* The word "our" teaches us we are to pray together, not just alone.

"Give us this day, our daily bread," teaches us to be dependent upon You, Father, for every need. Let us know and understand we can do nothing in and of ourselves. Every day we are dependent upon You.

Your death, burial, and resurrection paid for our debts, sins, and trespasses. How can we not forgive others when You, the blameless Lamb of God, not only forgave us, but paid the penalty for our sins? John 10:10 tells us, *"The thief came to steal, kill and destroy but You came that we might have life and might have it abundantly."*

We ask that You deliver us from the evil one. Protect us. Let us be wise like Joseph and flee from evil (Genesis 39:12). Yours is the kingdom, power, and glory, forever. You are the only one capable of creating the heavens and the earth. Only You can bring in Your kingdom of righteousness as laid out in Your Word. You are the only one capable of having Your glory last forever. We are Your children. Let us always glorify Your name. Let us pray with power, with confidence, with reverence, and with obedience to You who sustains our lives and gives us life eternal.

1 John 5:14, *"This is the confidence which we have before Him, that, if we ask anything according to His will, He hears us."* Thank You, Father, for hearing us today.

In the mighty name of Jesus.

Marta E Greenman   *Maureen H Maldonado*

REFLECTION

Review Matthew 6:1-8

1. How did Jesus tell them to NOT pray? (v. 7)

   _____
   _____
   _____

2. What can we be confident that our Father knows? (v. 8)

   _____
   _____
   _____

3. The basic outline of the Lord's Prayer is:

   v 9 honoring Him
   v 10 finding His will
   v 11 asking for our daily needs
   v 12 asking for and extending forgiveness
   v 13 deliverance from evil

   Which section of the Lord's prayer do you find most difficult and why?

   _____
   _____
   _____
   _____
   _____

PRAYER

Write your Lord's prayer:

DAY 21
PRAYING THE FATHER'S WILL

"³⁹ And He went a little beyond them, and fell on His face and prayed, saying, "My Father, if it is possible, let this cup pass from Me; yet not as I will, but as You wilt." ⁴⁰ And He came to the disciples and found them sleeping, and said to Peter, "So, you men could not keep watch with Me for one hour? ⁴¹ Keep watching and praying that you may not enter into temptation; the spirit is willing, but the flesh is weak." ⁴² He went away again a second time and prayed, saying, "My Father, if this cannot pass away unless I drink it, Thy will be done.""

Matthew 26:39-42

CONTEXT

Jesus knew His fate. Although He was fully God, He was also fully human. He knew that in a few hours, He would fulfill His purpose of coming to earth. The Roman means of punishment was crucifixion. When a person was nailed to a cross, the torture normally lasted three to four days before they finally died. To confirm someone had expired, a spear would be used to pierce a vital organ. Jesus knew this was His fate and He knew He needed to pray. He took three disciples to the garden. It has been said, He prayed so earnestly He perspired blood. Matthew 26:39 tells us He prayed, *"My Father, if it is possible, let this cup pass from Me; yet not as I will, but as Thy will."*

PRAYER

Father, God, I thank You that through Your Word, You show us we can come to You with any request. Just as Jesus asked to have the cup pass from Him, we too can ask for protection from any situation. It gives me confidence to know You are the God who hears and answers prayer. But as Jesus, we also need to pray, *"Your will be done, not mine."* We need to trust whatever happens is the best plan for eternity, Your plan.

Father, let us not be like the disciples who found themselves sleeping. Let us be alert and pray we may not enter into temptation, knowing the flesh is weak. As Jesus, when He prayed the second time in the garden, He knew Your will was to be fulfilled by His torture and death on the cross. He said, *"Thy will be done."* When we receive Your answers, and they are not our desire, give us strength to say, *"Thy will be done,"* regardless of the consequence.

Let us be keenly aware of our current times and be like David's men of valor and the Sons of Issachar, men who understood the times with knowledge of what they should do (1 Chronicles 12:32). Let us be men and women who understand the world around us. Remind us that we are called to be light in a dark place, revealing hope and the joy of salvation to all. We are to bear fruit to Christ's horrendous death and glorious resurrection.

Let us remember we need to surrender all our will to You. Your ways are greater than our ways. Your plans are better than our plans. Father, let us present our bodies as holy and living sacrifices. *"And do not be conformed to this world, but be transformed by the renewing of your mind, that you may prove what the will of God is, that which is good and acceptable and perfect"* (Romans 12:2).

Father, let us always remember it is, not as I will, but as You will.

In the mighty name of Jesus.

Marta E Greenman   *Maureen H Maldonado*

REFLECTION

Review Matthew 26:36-57

1. What did Jesus ask his disciples to do? (v. 36)

   _____
   _____
   _____
   _____

2. How did Peter, James, and John feel? (v. 37) Jesus knew His fate. What does Scripture tell us how He felt about this situation? (v. 38)

   _____
   _____
   _____
   _____

3. Jesus prayed for His Father's will to be done. What does this tell about Jesus? (vv. 39, 42, 44)

   _____
   _____
   _____
   _____
   _____

PRAYER

Write your prayer for paying the Father's will:

_____
_____
_____
_____
_____
_____
_____
_____
_____
_____
_____
_____
_____
_____
_____
_____
_____
_____
_____
_____

DAY 22
PRAYER FOR THE PERSECUTED AND THE PERSECUTOR

"¹¹And the Lord said to him, 'Arise and go to the street called Straight, and inquire at the house of Judas for a man from Tarsus named Saul, for behold, he is praying, ¹² and he has seen in a vision a man named Ananias come in and lay his hands on him, so that he might regain his sight."

Acts 9:11-12

CONTEXT

Time: Less than a year after Pentecost

Acts 7:58 tells us Saul (Paul) watched as Stephen became the first Christian to be martyred. Saul even held the coats of the participants who stoned Stephen and watched him die. After Stephen's death, Saul went into homes of believers and took them away to prison (Acts 8:2). As a result of the persecution, the church scattered throughout Judea and Samaria. Saul requested letters from the high priest for the synagogues in Damascus. He would travel there and seize Christians to return them in chains to Jerusalem (Acts 9:1-2). While on this murderous mission, Saul met Jesus. This encounter began his journey from the persecutor to one of the persecuted, who would eventually be martyred for Jesus Christ in 68 AD.

PRAYER

Father, thank You for Your Word, especially the book of Acts. Without it we would not know the history of the first century church! We would not understand the cost of being Your witness, your disciple! Thank You for the great cloud of witnesses who stand cheering us on from above. Father let me be Your faithful witness. Let me, like Saul, speak boldly to everyone. Let me speak Your words of grace and truth. Let me speak with confidence and wisdom. Let those who hear know and understand I am Your servant, speaking Your words, like John the Baptist when he said, *"He must increase but I must decrease"* (John 3:30).

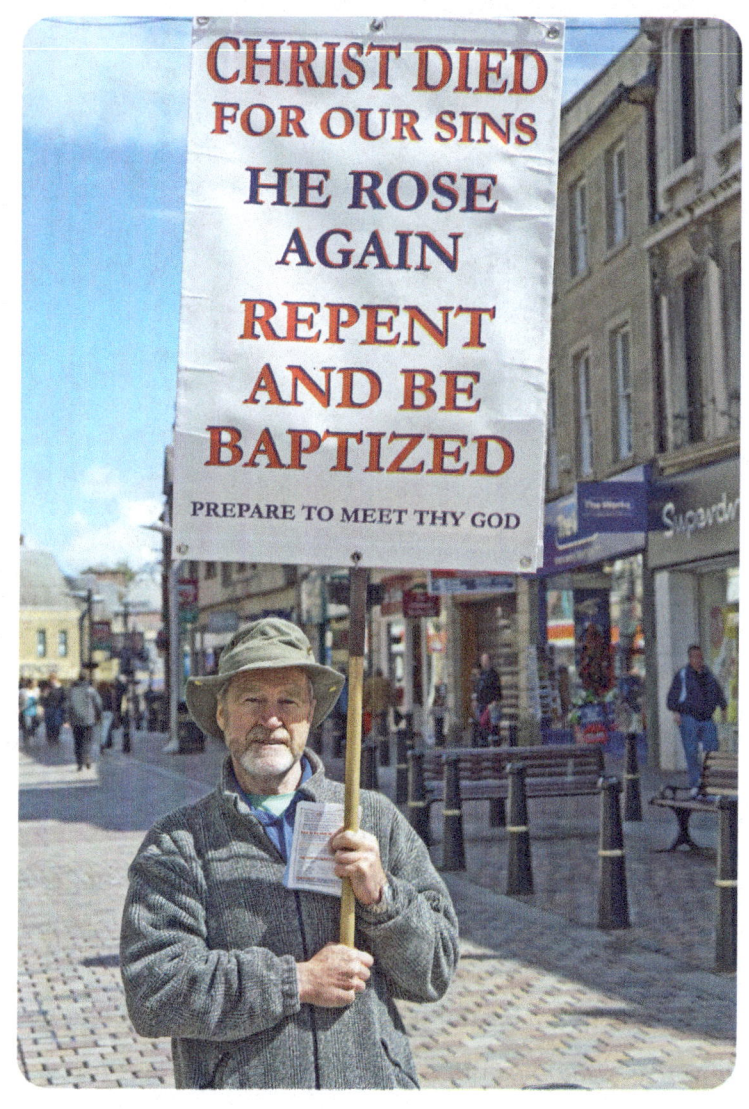

Today, more than 360 million Christians worldwide suffer severe persecution. Father, comfort them as only You can. Just as David prayed in Psalm 86:17, *"Show me a sign of good, that those who hate me may see it, and be ashamed, because Thou, O Lord, hast helped me and comforted me."* Strengthen the persecuted with Your righteous right hand. There are so many situations in which they can be fearful. Let them know YOU are their protector. Let them live by the words of Shadrach, Meshach, and Abed-nego, in Daniel 3:17-18, *"If it be so, our God whom we serve*

is able to deliver us from the furnace of blazing fire; and He will deliver us out of your hand, O king. But even if He does not, let it be known to you, O king, that we are not going to serve your gods or worship the golden image that you have set up."

Father, we pray for the persecutors! Your Word teaches, *"The Lord is not slow about His promise, as some count slowness, but is patient toward you, not wishing for any to perish but for all to come to repentance"* (2 Peter 3:9). Let them become powerhouse evangelists for Jesus Christ. Let them know they can be rescued from the pit of hell and have a purpose in the kingdom of God. Let them know they have a race to run for Jesus. *"Therefore, since we have so great a cloud of witnesses surrounding us, let us also lay aside every encumbrance, and the sin which so easily entangles us, and let us run with endurance the race that is set before us* (Hebrews 12:1). Let them be so passionate about the gospel and its transforming power that people will be compelled to acknowledge that only God could perform such a miracle in their lives and in doing so, turn to You for salvation.

Father, one day, *"At the name of Jesus every knee should bow, of those who are in heaven, and on earth, and under the earth, ¹¹ and that every tongue should confess that Jesus Christ is Lord, to the glory of God the Father"* (Philippians 2:10-11). Let that day begin today.

In the mighty name of Jesus.

REFLECTION

Review Matthew 26:36-57

1. What's your story? How did you come to believe that Jesus is the only one who can save you from your sins? Write your testimony below.

   _____
   _____
   _____
   _____
   _____

2. What was Ananias' response to the Lord when He told him to go to Saul? (v. 13)

   _____

3. What happened when Paul (Saul) proclaimed Jesus as the Christ (Anointed One/ Messiah)? (vv. 21-25)

   _____

4. What was the response of the believers in Jerusalem? (v. 26)

   _____

5. Who came to Paul's defense? What was the result? (v. 27)

   _____

6. What happened when the Hellenistic Jews heard Paul's bold speech for Jesus? (vv. 28-30)

   _____
   _____
   _____

PRAYER

Write your prayer for the persecuted and persecutor:

MY STORY
Somebody's Praying for Me

John G. Elliott wrote the song, *Somebody's Praying*. As someone who was raised in a Christian home with a strong heritage of believers, I've often wondered who was praying for me even before I was born! This question has frequently crossed my mind because of God's transformational power in my life. I know prayer had to be at the center of every miracle moment. My story is a modern-day Damascus Road experience.

When I finally surrendered my life to Christ, I was desperate to know Him and committed to learning God's Word for myself. I didn't want to know what man had to say about Him: I wanted to know what He had to say about Himself. These factors led me down a road to want others to know the greatness of God's mercy, love, and forgiveness. As a result, I found myself engaging in every opportunity to share the good news of the gospel. After several years of prison ministry, I heard of a mission trip to Romania and immediately knew I was to participate. With only five weeks to raise the funds, acquire my passport, and complete training, I boarded a 14-hour flight to Romania on Friday 13, 1997. The next ten days would change the trajectory of my life forever.

We were traveling to five areas of Eastern Romania. I was assigned to Seimeni, a small village in the Constanta region. This visit was the first time for this organization to minister in this area. The village included five hundred homes, one car, one telephone, and a post office. The first day I asked to stop by the post office for stamps. My translator looked at me like I was crazy and said, "They don't sell stamps at the post office!" I questioned, "What do they do at the post office?" She replied, "Once a month we come and pick up our mail." I was in for severe culture shock. Yet, it only took me about five minutes to fall in love with the people and ministry that was beginning.

While in Romania, I was reading through Acts. In chapter 9, Saul was traveling to Damascus with a letter from the High Priest to find believers and drag them back to Jerusalem for persecution. But on his journey, Saul had a profound encounter with Jesus on the road to Damascus. Saul's life was radically transformed in a moment. God directed Ananias to go to Saul. Ananias questioned the Lord, "Don't You know who he is?" (Marta paraphrase!) In Acts 9:15-16 the Lord replied to Ananias, *"Go, for he is a chosen instrument of Mine, to bear My name before the Gentiles and kings and the sons of Israel; for I will show him how much he must suffer for My name's sake."*

The moment I read those words, I knew God was speaking to me. The words leaped off the page and into my heart. My entire life made sense at that moment. After ten days of ministry, I returned home and announced to my husband that I wanted to leave my career and become a staff missionary. This meant I would raise my own support, travel out of the country several times a year on short-term mission trips, to tell people about Jesus, and help plant new churches. It is amazing to me how well my husband embraced the idea. That trip changed the direction of my life, our lives, forever. Twenty-five years later I see how God orchestrated each step to move me forward in the plans HE laid out for me before the foundation of the world.

I can't wait to get to heaven and find out all those who have been praying for me through all these years. Some are my precious friends who encourage me daily, like my dear friend Becky. From the moment we met 15 years ago, God impressed upon her to pray for me and my ministry daily. She awakes faithfully at 5 a.m. to pray for Words of Grace & Truth and my needs. Others I may never know of until I see them in eternity, but I know their prayers have impacted my life for His glory.

Marta E Greenman

DAY 23
PRAYER OF PRAISE

"²³ When they had inflicted many blows upon them, they threw them into prison, commanding the jailer to guard them securely; ²⁴ and he, having received such a command, threw them into the inner prison and fastened their feet in the stocks.²⁵ But about midnight Paul and Silas were praying and singing hymns of praise to God, and the prisoners were listening to them; ²⁶ and suddenly there came a great earthquake, so that the foundations of the prison house were shaken; and immediately all the doors were opened and everyone's chains were unfastened."

Acts 16:23-26

CONTEXT

The word "praise" in Acts 16:25 is the Greek word "*Humnēō*", used in only four Scriptures. Matthew 26:30 and Mark 14:26 describe the same event in each gospel. Just after the Passover when Jesus gave them the bread and the cup, Matthew 26:28 says, *"This is My blood of the covenant, which is poured out for many for forgiveness of sins."* Matthew 26:30 says, *"after singing a hymn (Humnēō), they went out to the Mount of Olives."*

The third mention is Hebrews 2:12 which quotes Psalm 22:22, *"In the midst of the congregation I will sing Thy praise,"* (*Humnēō*) speaking of Christ's death on the cross.

Acts 16:25 is the final allusion to *Humnēō* with Paul and Silas in chains while in prison. What do these four occasions have in common? These

are times of severe distress. But each time, the disciples sing praises joyfully in the midst of great tribulation (*Humnēō*).

Despite the seriousness of each situation, the men were able to sing praises to the living God. Even if we do not know the outcome, we are to *Humnēō* (praise) the Lord. Our God can perform miracles and raise the dead. But even if He does not, we will still praise Him.

PRAYER

Father, You are great and greatly to be praised. Let us always remember to praise (*Humnēō*) You regardless of the storms that surround us. The difficulties may be Your opportunity to show us miracles we could never behold otherwise. Just as the storms raged when Jesus and the disciples were in the boat, Jesus rebuked the winds, and the seas became perfectly calm. Let us know and understand Jesus is the One who will calm our fears while others will stand around and be amazed.

Let us humble and position ourselves for a miracle as in Biblical times. Father, we do not know whether You will part the seas, shut the mouth of the lion, raise the dead, or allow us to escape the edge of the sword. Every miracle is from You, and we must always give You praise, glory, and honor.

Just like the case of Paul and Silas, let others be a witness to the miracles You have done in our lives so they may believe in the One true living God. We pray they repent and turn to You. Let us also be diligent to make disciples and teach Your Word with truth and boldness, as Paul and Silas. May we never shrink away, no matter the persecution.

Paul and Silas were dragged before the authorities because lies were told about them. Let us know that the closer Your return to earth, persecution will increase. But, like Paul and Silas, let us be steadfast, unmovable, and unshakable in our faith and in our courage. Let us never cease to sing Your praise (*Humneō*) until we see You face-to-face.

In the mighty name of Jesus.

Marta E Greenman   *Maureen H Maldonado*

REFLECTION

Review Acts 16:14-34

1. Why were Paul and Silas imprisoned? (vv.16-19)

   _____
   _____

2. What was the result of Paul and Silas praying and singing hymns of praise *(Humnēō)* to God?

   _____
   _____

   v. 26

   _____
   _____

   v. 27

   _____
   _____

   vv. 28-31

   _____
   _____

3. Of the jailer's household, who was saved? (v. 34)

   _____
   _____
   _____

PRAYER

Write your prayer of praise *(Humnēō)*:

DAY 24
PRAYER FOR KNOWLEDGE AND SPRITUAL WISDOM

"⁹For this reason also, since the day we heard of it, we have not ceased to pray for you and to ask that you may be filled with the knowledge of His will in all spiritual wisdom and understanding, ¹⁰so that you will walk in a manner worthy of the Lord, to please Him in all respects, bearing fruit in every good work and increasing in the knowledge of God; ¹¹strengthened with all power, according to His glorious might, for the attaining of all steadfastness and patience; joyously ¹²giving thanks to the Father, who has qualified us to share in the inheritance of the saints in Light."

Colossians 1:9-12

CONTEXT

Paul wrote this letter to the church in Colossae while bound in chains in prison (approximately 62 AD). People, including the Jews, flocked to Colossae because it was on a major trade route. The city was considered the home of Oriental mysticism. Even though Paul had never met those believers, his heart yearned for that church to be rooted in the truth of God's Word. He wanted them to practice sound doctrine, not the new-age ideas of the Orient. Paul addressed the church as saints and faithful brethren. He reported he had never stopped praying for them since he had heard about this new body of believers.

PRAYER

Father, I want to be a man/woman of God who is filled with Your knowledge, spiritual wisdom, and understanding. My heart's desire is to walk in a manner worthy of You, Lord. Let me daily study Your Word, not to be puffed up or arrogant, but to have and desire an intimate relationship with You that changes my life. We know Bible study is about *transformation,* NOT information. Let Your knowledge and spiritual wisdom make me more like You and less like me. Let Your transforming work penetrate my life and heart day by day so I might bear more fruit.

Let me be like the one with five talents and turn them into ten talents for Your glory alone (Matthew 25:14-30). I long for the results of Your Word as Paul described; let me be a glorious light to the nations and draw people to Your saving grace and eternal life. I do ask to attain steadfastness like Paul and patience like Abraham to wait for what You have promised (Genesis 21:5).

Let me always give thanks in all things, during good times and times of tribulation. Let me, like James, in James 1:2-4, *"Consider it all joy, my brethren, when you encounter various trials, knowing that the testing of your faith produces endurance. And let endurance have its perfect result, that you may be perfect and complete, lacking in nothing."*

I need endurance, Father; I need to be complete and lack nothing. Let Your Word penetrate my heart that I might memorize it and always recall it. Psalms 1:2-3 teaches, *"His delight is in the law of the Lord, And in His law he meditates day and night. And he will be like a tree firmly planted by streams of water, which yields its fruit in its season, and its leaf does not wither; and in whatever he does, he prospers."* I want to delight in Your Word; I want to meditate on it day and night. I want to yield fruit in season. Let my life please You and You alone. You are God, King of kings, Lord of lords, and I am Your servant.

In the mighty name of Jesus.

REFLECTION

Review Colossians 1:9-12

1. What did Paul ask from the Lord? To be filled with:

   _____
   _____
   _____
   _____

2. Why did Paul ask for knowledge, spiritual wisdom, and understanding? What would the result become?

   _____
   _____
   _____
   _____

3. How do you think your life would change if you prayed Paul's prayer to Colossae for yourself and others, and if you received the same results?

   _____
   _____
   _____
   _____

PRAYER

Write your prayer of Knowledge and Spiritual Wisdom:

ATTITUDINAL PRAYERS

Some passages in Scripture imply prayer, but the word prayer is not used. For example, John 17:1, *"These things Jesus spoke; and lifting up His eyes to heaven, He said, . . ."* This is a clear indication Jesus was praying to the Father. Another example is Psalm 51:1-2, *"Be gracious to me, O God, according to Thy lovingkindness; according to the greatness of Thy compassion blot out my transgressions. Wash me thoroughly from my iniquity, and cleanse me from my sin."* David wrote this Psalm after He sinned with Bathsheba. David asking the Lord to cleanse him from sin is a prayer of repentance. These prayers are called Attitudinal Prayers. The remainder of our prayers in the New Testament are Attitudinal Prayers; they are within the following texts:

Luke 23:34 – *"But Jesus was saying, 'Father, forgive them; for they do not know what they are doing.' And they cast lots, dividing up His garments among themselves."*

John 17:1-10, 11-16, 17-19, 20-26 the High Priestly Prayer – *"These things Jesus spoke; and lifting up His eyes to heaven, He said, . . ."*

Revelation 22:20 – *"He who testifies to these things says, 'Yes, I am coming quickly.' Amen. Come, Lord Jesus."*

DAY 25
PRAYER OF FORGIVENESS

"But Jesus was saying, 'Father, forgive them; for they do not know what they are doing.' And they cast lots, dividing up His garments among themselves."

Luke 23:34

CONTEXT

Just one week earlier the crowds brought palms and waved them to honor Jesus as He rode into the city on a donkey. That same crowd took Jesus to Pilate to be crucified. Because the crowd cried for the third time, *"Crucify Him, Crucify Him,"* Pilate was compelled to release the murderer Barabbas and to deliver Jesus to the crowd. Jesus

was taken to the place called The Skull, Calvary, where they crucified Him. While hanging on the cross, Luke 23:34 tells us, *"But Jesus was saying, 'Father, forgive them; for they do not know what they are doing.' And they cast lots, dividing up His garments among themselves."*

PRAYER

In Psalm 63:1b, Lord, You tell us, *"My soul thirsts for Thee, my flesh yearns for Thee, in a dry and weary land where there is no water."* Unforgiveness is like that dry and weary land. It brings bitterness, anger, anxiety, depression, and even fear. It becomes like a poison that invades our bodies. Nelson Mandella said, "Unforgiveness is like drinking the poison and expecting the other person to die."

Father, I want my soul to be right and in communion with You. Unforgiveness hinders the relationship with God and man. It rubs off like poison to other people.

In Mark 11:25, You tell us, as we forgive others, You will also forgive us. Lord, I NEED Your forgiveness, every single day.

Father, teach us through your Word to forgive, even in the most difficult circumstances. Let me have Your heart to love those who cast insults and those who might want to harm me. The world has become an ugly place where it is every person for himself no matter what. Love thy neighbor was once the norm, and people respected one another's differences. Let me set the example, and even when backbiting and slander come my way, let me pray, *"Father, forgive them for they know not what they are doing"* (Luke 23:34). In doing so, may people come to know You as Lord and Savior and let Your name be glorified above all nations.

Marta E Greenman   *Maureen H Maldonado*

REFLECTION

Review Luke 23:34

1. Under what circumstance was Jesus asking His Father to forgive?

   _____
   _____
   _____
   _____
   _____

2. Has there been a time when you were unfairly judged? Describe the process you used for forgiveness.

   _____
   _____
   _____
   _____
   _____

3. What were the positive outcomes of forgiveness (for you? ... for the other?)

   _____
   _____
   _____
   _____
   _____

PRAYER

Write your prayer of forgiveness:

DAY 26, 27, 28, 29
HIGH PRIESTLY PRAYER

CONTEXT

High Priestly Prayer Days 26, 27, 28, 29

The book of John was written to testify of the signs (miracles) Jesus performed, *"But these have been written that you may believe that Jesus is the Christ, the Son of God; and that believing you may have life in His name"* (John 20:31). Yet chapter 13 throughout the end of the book focuses specifically on the last week of Jesus' life, crucifixion, resurrection, and meeting the disciples after His resurrection.

John 17 is known as the High Priestly Prayer; some may say the *Farewell Prayer*. It is the longest recorded prayer of Jesus and His final prayer before Judas' betrayal and being handed over to the Roman guards. John 13 through 17 record the final Feast of the Passover. Jesus was at His "Last Supper" with His disciples. He washed their feet and prophesied His betrayal by Judas. Later He promised His disciples He would not leave them as orphans, but would send a Helper, the Holy Spirit (John 14:18). Jesus gave His *I Am the Vine* sermon. He instructed the disciples how they should treat one another and how they should regard the world, no matter how the world would treat them. In John 16, He reiterated the promise of the Holy Spirit and told of His impending crucifixion. John 17 tells us that Jesus raised His head toward heaven and prayed what we know today as the High Priestly Prayer.

In the next four days, we will analyze Jesus' prayer. We have divided it into three sections — glorification, sanctification, and unification.

DAY 26
PRAYER OF GLORIFICATION

HIGH PRIESTLY PRAYER PART 1 (ESV)

"¹ When Jesus had spoken these words, he lifted up his eyes to heaven, and said, "Father, the hour has come; glorify your Son that the Son may glorify you, ² since you have given him authority over all flesh, to give eternal life to all whom you have given him. ³ And this is eternal life, that they know you, the only true God, and Jesus Christ whom you have sent. ⁴ I glorified you on earth, having accomplished the work that you gave me to do. ⁵ And now, Father, glorify me in your own presence with the glory that I had with you before the world existed. ⁶ "I have manifested your name to the people whom you gave me out of the world. Yours they were, and you gave them to me, and they have kept your word. ⁷ Now they know that everything that you have given me is from you. ⁸ For I have given them the words  *that you gave me, and they have received them and have come to know in truth that I came from you; and they have believed that you sent me. ⁹ I am praying for them. I am not praying for the world but for those whom you have given me, for they are yours. ¹⁰ All mine are yours, and yours are mine, and I am glorified in them."*

John 17:1-10 (ESV)

CONTEXT

Refer to page 226.

PRAYER

Father, You glorify Your Son and Your Son glorifies You. You gave Jesus authority over all mankind and eternal life can be attained only through Him. He glorified You in accomplishing the work which You gave Him. Father, we ask that we glorify You and the work You prepared for us (Ephesians 2:10). Just as Jesus, we are in the world, but not of the world (John 17:16).

You sent us Your Spirit to guide us to truth and to disclose what is to come (John 16:13). The Spirit glorifies You, Jesus, by disclosing Your will to us. By doing Your will, we glorify You and glorify the Father.

We ask that You be present in all aspects of our lives - family, business, personal, and relationships. How we treat everyone we encounter is an indication of our relationship with You. We ask that love, joy, peace, patience, kindness, goodness, faithfulness, gentleness, and self-control flow from You through us into everyone with whom we have contact.

Father, the sacrifice of Your Son, Jesus, on the cross made eternal life available to all mankind. We must individually accept this gift by faith. We are saved by Your grace, by our faith, for good works (Ephesians 2:8-10). Salvation is not attained by good works, but good works have been predestined for us after we have been saved.

Father, set us apart and keep us from the world to do good works. We have good works to do, but we cannot do them until we are saved. We know good works do not save us, but they are an earthly result of our salvation so we may glorify our Father in heaven.

Father, show us what You have for us to do so we may glorify You.

In the mighty name of Jesus.

Marta E Greenman *Maureen H Maldonado*

REFLECTION

Review John 17:1-10

1. What does verse 2 teach us about Jesus' relationship to man?

   _____

   _____

2. Eternal life can only be attained by going through whom?

   _____

   _____

3. How did Jesus glorify God on earth? (v. 4)

   _____

   _____

4. Who gave the disciples to Jesus and what did they do? (vv. 6-7)

   _____

   _____

5. Who did the disciples believe sent Jesus to earth?

   _____

   _____

6. Based on verse 10, how was Jesus glorified?

   _____

   _____

   _____

PRAYER

Write your prayer of honoring and glorifying God with your life:

DAY 27
PRAYER OF PRESERVATION

HIGH PRIESTLY PRAYER PART 2 (ESV)

"11 And I am no longer in the world, but they are in the world, and I am coming to you. Holy Father, keep them in your name, which you have given me, that they may be one, even as we are one. 12 While I was with them, I kept them in your name, which you have given me. I have guarded them, and not one of them has been lost except the son of destruction, that the Scripture might be fulfilled. 13 But now I am coming to you, and these things I speak in the world, that they may have my joy fulfilled in themselves. 14 I have given them your word, and the world has hated them because they are not of the world, just as I am not of the world. 15 I do not ask that you take them out of the world, but that you keep them from the evil one. 16 They are not of the world, just as I am not of the world."

John 17:11-16 (ESV)

CONTEXT

Refer to page 226.

PRAYER

Thank you, Lord, for Your example of the Father/Son relationship. Your word tells us in John 17:11, Your desire is for believers to be as one just as the Father, Son, and Holy Spirit are One. The absence of unity in the body of Christ is evidence we are failing our responsibility. The Church seems to be more divided today than ever. We humbly ask for Your forgiveness, and that You will show us ways in which we can help unify the body of Christ. We pray that You continue to guard us and keep us.

I am thankful for Your words in John 10:27-28, *"'My sheep hear My voice, and I know them, and they follow Me; and I give eternal life to them, and they shall never perish; and no one shall snatch them out of My hand."* We can confidently and boldly walk forward in this turbulent world because Your grip is firmly upon us. Even when the world hates us, we can have joy in this unstable world. We know we will have tribulation, but we will not worry because You have overcome the world (John 16:33). Let us not be surprised when we are hated because of Your name. Instead, we pray the words of Paul in Ephesians 4:1, *"I therefore, the prisoner of the Lord, entreat you to walk in a manner worthy of the calling with which you have been called."*

Finally, Father, You tell us we are not of the world. Show us daily how to live a life pleasing to You while on this earth. Let us be an example so others will know we are Yours and You are ours. We pray 2 Thessalonians 3:3, *"But the Lord is faithful, and He will strengthen and protect you from the evil one."* This was Your prayer for us so please remind us daily to join with You in praying for our protection.

In the might name of Jesus.

REFLECTION

Review John 17:11-16

1. In John 17:1-10, the focus is on Jesus' relationship with God. In John 17:11-16, on whom is the focus?

   _____
   _____
   _____

2. What was Jesus' request to His Father regarding the disciples?

   _____
   _____
   _____
   _____

3. Why will the world hate believers?

   _____
   _____
   _____
   _____

4. What does it mean to be "in the world but not of this world?"

   _____
   _____
   _____
   _____

PRAYER

Write your prayer of preservation:

DAY 28
PRAYER OF SANCTIFICATION
HIGH PRIESTLY PRAYER PART 3 (ESV)

"¹⁷ Sanctify them in the truth; your word is truth. ¹⁸ As you sent me into the world, so I have sent them into the world. ¹⁹ And for their sake I consecrate myself, that they also may be sanctified in truth."

John 17:17-19 (ESV)

CONTEXT

Refer to page 226.

PRAYER

Father, I thank You that Your desire is to sanctify us. Philippians 1:6 tells us, *"For I am confident of this very thing, that He who began a good work in you will perfect it until the day of Christ Jesus."* What a comfort this is to me knowing You began the work and You will finish the work. Sanctification is You setting us apart from the world for Your purposes. You take us as we are and turn us into whom You created us to be before sin entered the world. Like the metamorphosis of a butterfly, we start as one image and the final result is a beautiful tapestry of someone only You could design.

The purpose of sanctification is to prepare us for our earthly assignment. In Ephesians 2:10 we are told, *"For we are His workmanship, created in Christ Jesus for good works, which God prepared beforehand, that we should walk in them."* Sanctification will allow us to go about Your business. It is not just doing what we are called, but doing them in a manner pleasing to You, Lord. The sanctification process will make us more like You. We will love like You. We will have joy like You. We can have the peace that passes all understanding, like You. We will have patience beyond our human ability like You. We will be kind to those who are unkind, like You. We will have the goodness of the Father, with His patience, peace, and kindness.

In Hebrews 12:10, we are told, *"For they (fathers) disciplined us for a short time as seemed best to them, but He (God) disciplines us for our good, that we may share His holiness."* We are to be holy as You are holy (Leviticus 19:20). Our heart's desire is to be like You. Without discipline we will never learn what is necessary to be Your faithful child. Thank you, Father, for doing whatever it takes to bring us closer to You.

In the mighty name of Jesus.

Marta E Greenman   *Maureen H Maldonado*

REFLECTION

Review John 17:11-19

1. How would you define sanctification?

   _____
   _____
   _____
   _____
   _____

2. How does God tell us to be sanctified?

   _____
   _____
   _____
   _____
   _____
   _____

3. Give examples of how God has been sanctifying you.

   _____
   _____
   _____
   _____
   _____
   _____
   _____

PRAYER

Write your prayer of sanctification:

DAY 29
PRAYER OF UNIFICATION
HIGH PRIESTLY PRAYER PART 4 (ESV)

"²⁰ I do not ask for these only, but also for those who will believe in me through their word, ²¹ that they may all be one, just as you, Father, are in me, and I in you, that they also may be in us, so that the world may believe that you have sent me. ²² The glory that you have given me I have given to them, that they may be one even as we are one, ²³ I in them and you in me, that they may become perfectly one, so that the world may know that you sent me and loved them even as you loved me. ²⁴ Father, I desire that they also, whom you have given me, may be with me where I am, to see my glory that you have given me because you loved me before the foundation of the world. ²⁵ O righteous Father, even though the world does not know you, I know you, and these know that you have sent me. ²⁶ I made known to them your name, and I will continue to make it known, that the love with which you have loved me may be in them, and I in them."

John 17:20-26 (ESV)

CONTEXT

Refer to page 226.

PRAYER

Father, before sin entered the world, man had a one-on-one relationship with You. Because of the fall of man, that relationship became broken. Thank You that You always want fellowship with Your people, but not until Jesus' death and resurrection was our relationship restored. Now we go directly to the High Priest rather than a mediator who would sacrifice animals and offer up prayers on our behalf. When Jesus became our once and for all sacrifice, Your promise was fulfilled. The Comforter, Helper, Holy Spirit, then came so we would have a permanent, open communication line with You. We are thankful You want to have

this close relationship. Father, I pray not only for unity between You and me, but for unity among all believers. Only You can perfect us in unity. This will be how the world will know that we are Yours. Father, let us show Your love to the world so they too may come to know You.

Father, You tell us in 1 John 4:7, *"Beloved, let us love one another, for love is from God; and everyone who loves is born of God and knows God."* In 1 John 4:10 You say, *"In this is love, not that we loved God but that He loved us and sent His son to be the propitiation (appeasement of God's just judgment) for our sins."* You are our example of loving the unlovable because You loved us first. Let us be that example to the world, drawing people to You so they too may know Your love and forgiveness.

In the mighty name of Jesus.

Marta E Greenman   *Maureen H Maldonado*

REFLECTION

Review John 17:20-26

1. Why did God send Jesus to earth?

   - (v. 21) _____

   - (v. 24) _____

   - (v. 26) _____

2. How can we display unity within the Church to reach the world?

   _____
   _____
   _____
   _____
   _____

3. In what ways can we show God's love to others, believers, and non-believers?

   _____
   _____
   _____
   _____
   _____

PRAYER

Write your prayer of unity:

MY STORY
Praying Unites Our Souls

Many years ago, I was part of a team of women who went weekly into a private state jail in downtown Dallas to minister to incarcerated women. Every week we would gather and pray for these precious women we would soon encounter. It was a wonderful time of ministry even before we ever entered the jail.

We were assigned to three different pods. A pod was a cell block of 54 women who lived together. The women from the church would have a time of worship music, a devotional or Bible study, and then prayer with whomever was in need. One of the pods was called the God pod. These women had earned the right to stay in this pod because of their good behavior and other criteria. They also had various classes, often biblical. The women stayed busy each day and we were blessed to be a part of their weekly schedule.

On one of our visits, I met a beautiful young woman named Kimberlyn. As with most, Kimberlyn was incarcerated on drugs charges. I remember her beautiful smile and sweet spirit. I was very surprised she was there since she didn't seem to "fit in" with the rest. The day I had the opportunity to meet her, Kimberlyn spoke of nothing but her children, and we prayed for their protection and their hearts. It was obvious to me that she loved Jesus. I had plenty of prison ministry experience and was not naive to the recidivism rates of those incarcerated, but I remember feeling confident for Kimberlyn once released, she would not return to prison.

We noted the names of women and circumstances of the women so we could pray for them throughout the week. Kimberlyn was only there for six months, so it wasn't long before she was gone. And due to rules, we were not allowed to keep in touch.
About two years later, my husband Marshall, and I were helping with a church plant in south Dallas. One day after church, we stopped by a local restaurant for lunch and Kimberlyn was our hostess! I knew God had ordained this meeting. She remembered me and we had a blessed

reunion. Marshall and I stopped there almost every week after that so I could see and talk to Kimberlyn. I was excited to hear she was in church. Christmas was coming and she was making plans to see her children. Once again, we prayed for her children and their hearts. We prayed for Kimberlyn's relationship with them to be strengthened. From that moment, we have remained in touch. I've had the privilege of seeing God grow and mature her into a beautiful woman of God. I heard of the restored relationship and reunion with her children. In 2015 she married a godly man and they have been faithful to the Lord and to each other.

In January 2020, Kimberlyn was diagnosed with cancer, and has been battling ever since. Kimberlyn is on a long list of people I know personally who are battling various kinds of cancer. Some have begun to win the battle, while some have already beat me to the King and are now with Jesus face-to-face. But I pray daily for the Lord to heal each and every one of them. What an opportunity the Lord has given me to be involved in this precious woman's life through prayer. God has knit our hearts together as only He can. Paul wrote in Philippians 1:7, *"For it is only right for me to feel this way about you all, because I have you in my heart, since both in my imprisonment and in the defense and confirmation of the gospel, you all are partakers of grace with me."* This is what prayer can do. I pray you have many Kimberlyn's in your life for which you have the privilege to pray and see God work miracles before your very eyes.

Marta E Greenman

Kimberlyn Michelle Stone closed her eyes in her earthly home on April 27, 2024, but because Kimberlyn placed her faith in Jesus Christ in 2012, she immediately reopened her eyes in the presence of her Lord and was ushered into her Heavenly home.

DAY 30
PRAYER FOR JERUSALEM

"He who testifies to these things says, 'Yes, I am coming quickly.' Amen. Come, Lord Jesus."

Revelation 22:20

CONTEXT

Psalm 122:6a instructs us, *"Pray for the peace of Jerusalem."* This verse is intertwined with the closing statement in Revelation because they are communicating the same message. In

Revelation, Jesus says, *"I am coming quickly."* When we pray for the peace of Jerusalem, we are praying for Jesus to come quickly! In a world that is being turned upside down, it is important to pray for the return of Our Lord daily. Please understand, the Bible is quite clear, the closer the return of Jesus, the more turbulent the days will become. We must be diligent to pray for the Lord's return and for the peace of Jerusalem.

PRAYER

Father, You made the heavens and the earth. You spoke the world into existence. You laid the foundations of the earth. The heavens are the works of Your hands. You created us in Your image and likeness, (Genesis 1:26). You are King over all creation. You have appointed a time for Your return, but not even Your Son knows the day or the hour (Matthew 24:36). 1 Thessalonians 5:4 tells us, *"But you, brethren, are not in darkness, that the day should overtake you like a thief."* This

verse teaches as believers we are ready for the day of the coming of Jesus Christ. However, naysayers will mockingly say, "When is the Lord's return?" Just as in the days of Noah, they will mock and make fun of the Lord. Let this not escape their notice, a Day of Judgment is coming. The signs of the time are all around us. We are to be ever watchful, waiting. We must stay alert. Our duty until You return is to pray and make known, with boldness, the mystery of the gospel (Ephesians 6:19).

Matthew 24:6-8 teaches, *"'And you will be hearing of wars and rumors of wars; see that you are not frightened, for those things must take place, but that is not yet the end. For nation will rise against nation, and kingdom against kingdom, and in various places there will be famines and earthquakes. But all these things are merely the beginning of birth pangs."* Lord, we understand between now and the time of Your return, we will have difficult times. We should expect trials and tribulations. James 1:12 teaches, *"Blessed is a man who perseveres under trial; for once he has been approved, he will receive the crown of life, which the Lord has promised to those who love Him."* Let us diligently run the race You have given us, knowing the world will not understand. And in most instances, we will be in direct conflict with the world. Let us acquire the mindset of Peter and the apostles when they were summoned before the Council in Acts 5:41, *"So they went on their way from the presence of the Council, rejoicing that they had been considered worthy to suffer shame for His name."*

In the mighty name of Jesus.

Marta E Greenman   *Maureen H Maldonado*

REFLECTION

Review Revelation 22:20 and Psalm 122:6a

1. What are you doing to prepare for the return of Christ?

   _____
   _____
   _____
   _____
   _____

2. What are you doing to prepare others, including your family, for the return of Christ?

   _____
   _____
   _____
   _____
   _____
   _____

3. Do you persevere under trial? Give examples.

   _____
   _____
   _____
   _____
   _____

PRAYER

Write your prayer for Jerusalem:

YOUR STORY

We want to know what God has done in your life!
Write your testimony here or send an email to info@wogt.org.

If this devotional ministered to you, please let us know where you purchased the book, leave a review on Amazon, and recommend it to your friends and family.

Thank you.

Follow us on social media:

Facebook - Words of Grace & Truth
Instagram – WordsOfGraceandTruth
Linkedin - Marta Greenman
Linkedin - Maureen Maldonado
Twitter - MartaEGreenman@WordsGraceTruth
TikTok – MartaEGreenman

Contact us:

Words of Grace & Truth
PO Box 860223
Plano, TX 75086
info@wogt.org
469-854-3574

Words of Grace & Truth is sustained by faithful ministry partners. Would you consider making a tax-deductible donation? Visit us at www.wogt.org and click the Donate Now button at the top right hand of the page.

Made in the USA
Coppell, TX
06 February 2026